MAY 2 2

ALSO BY GARY JANETTI

*Do You Mind If I Cancel?*
*(Things That Still Annoy Me)*

# start *without* me

# start *without* me

(I'll Be There in a Minute)

## GARY JANETTI

Henry Holt and Company
New York

Henry Holt and Company
*Publishers since 1866*
120 Broadway
New York, New York 10271
www.henryholt.com

Henry Holt® and ⒽⓇ are registered trademarks of Macmillan
Publishing Group, LLC.

Library of Congress Cataloging-in-Publication Data is available

ISBN: 9781250225856

Our books may be purchased in bulk for promotional,
educational, or business use. Please contact your local
bookseller or the Macmillan Corporate and Premium Sales
Department at (800) 221-7945, extension 5442, or by e-mail at
MacmillanSpecialMarkets@macmillan.com.

First Edition 2022

Designed by Meryl Sussman Levavi

Printed in the United States of America

1   3   5   7   9   10   8   6   4   2

*For Brad*
*and for*
*Mom, Dad and Maria*

# Contents

# start *without* me

# The
# Carol Burnett
# Show

I'M NINE YEARS OLD. I LIVE IN QUEENS. (A PLACE I wanted to get out of so badly but now revisit in my mind almost daily.) It is summer and it is hot and it is sticky and the basement is where I spend most of my day. Watching TV in the underground coolness. My mother desperate for me to go outside. Leave the house, it is summer. I'm supposed to be outside. I pray each morning for it to rain. It never does. (Ironically, in later life I become fixated every summer on it *not* raining, each vacation destination planned for optimal sunshine probability. A trip in my thirties to Provincetown with five straight days of rain is something that still makes me sick to my stomach. Gay people are obsessed with the summer. Preparing for it with the kind of ferocious dedication usually reserved for Olympians.)

I was sent to day camp when I was seven. Getting on a bus with other kids and taken to some local park that was five minutes away but might as well have been South Dakota. Sickly sweet orange drinks handed out from cardboard boxes. And kids would take one and then waltz right up to each other and start talking. Just like that. Like the most nightmarish tiny cocktail party you could imagine. And then they would run or jump or throw a ball or some other terrible thing. I would've sooner walked out into the middle of the Long Island Expressway and opened a lawn chair before I joined them.

There was one counselor that I liked, though. She was the wife of a man my father knew from his job as a salesman for Cunard Cruise Line. Rose had black hair she wore to her shoulders and seemed impossibly cosmopolitan to me because she carried a PBS tote bag. In the '70s that was as close as I was going to come to a safe space. Each day I would take my orange drink and walk up to Rose, who was usually reading a paperback while infrequently glancing up at the kids, and sit with her. I was never more relaxed than when I was with a woman over thirty reading a book. "Don't you want to play with the other kids?" she'd ask. "I don't," I'd respond. Eventually she stopped asking.

"So what's new? What are you reading?" I'd say as I sidled up next to her on the picnic table bench. (I was good at making small talk with anyone twenty-five-years or more older than me. A fellow child was like something from another planet. But a married woman with sunglasses and a cigarette was my kind of company.)

Rose and I would chat each day. She would tell me what she was cooking for dinner that night, what she was watching on TV, small things that maybe she told nobody else. (My little gay seven-year-old self already practicing for what would be years of listening to women talk about their problems, until I got to the age when I was able to have my own relationships and then would inevitably force them to listen to *my* much more embellished, overly dramatic ones. These tables turn usually overnight for all gay men and their closest female friend. We learn from them and then we take what we learn and we raise the stakes exponentially.)

I would look forward to seeing Rose. I suddenly wasn't going to day camp but rather was taking a bus to meet with my dearest girlfriend. In a kinder world, one that didn't frown on relationships between seven-year-old gay boys and thirty-year-old married women, we'd be getting coffees on our way to yoga instead of sitting on damp grass watching fat kids play Wiffle ball.

My mother was happy that I now seemed to enjoy camp. She would quiz me on what I was doing there and I would respond noncommittally, "Stuff." She never pressed too hard, so relieved was she that I would finally leave the house without a meltdown that could rival Olivia de Havilland in *The Snake Pit*.

Weeks pass uneventfully until one day my mother asks me why I spend all my time with Rose and won't play with the other kids. Rose is concerned, my mother tells me. And this is my first taste of betrayal. Here I was thinking we were having a lovely summer together, Rose and I, only to find out that she saw me as nothing more than some child. Some friendless kid who didn't know how to throw a ball. Some nobody. Gay people, even at the tender age of seven, know how to turn against someone in the most chilling of fashions. Damien in *The Omen* didn't give as dead-eyed a stare as I did the next time I saw her. "Good morning," I said, with the inflection of a corpse. I think she might have even gasped, so bitchy was my demeanor. A stark contrast from the chummy *Laverne & Shirley* roles I'd previously cast us in. My carefree smiles and easy laugh now replaced with the expressionless mask of a sociopath. "I'll take my juice now, please," was the last thing I ever said to Rose.

The following summer, when I'm eight, on the first day of camp, I hide my bus pass in a jar of peanut butter. My mother scrambling to find it as I casually leaf through *TV Guide*, planning my day. "It was right here!" she says, frustrated as she scans our compact kitchen again. "Well, I guess I can't go," I say. "What did you do with it?" she asks, suddenly on to me. "Nothing. Now if you'll excuse me, I'll be in the basement watching *Double Indemnity*."

But she insists, I must have done something with it. I shrug. I'll go to my grave buried with that jar of peanut butter before I confess. "Well, come on, we're going!" "I can't go without a bus pass!" "Yes, you can, I'll explain it to the driver." What the fuck was this woman's fixation on sending me to camp? The only way she was going to get me onto that bus was in a straitjacket. "I'm not going." She looked at me, almost pleading, "Don't you want to play with the other kids outside? It's summer." Was I not the same child that she had had for the previous eight years? Had I ever *once* played outside? "I want to watch TV downstairs." And she let me go. This was the hill I was willing to die on, and she knew it.

I thought that was going to be the end of it. But it wasn't. The following year, as I'm almost finished suffering through the countless humiliations of third grade, two months alone in front of the basement TV now so close I can taste it, my parents tell me they have a proposition for me.

"What?" I ask, suspicious.

"How about if we send you to sleepaway camp this summer?" If they had snapped our cat's neck in front of me I would've been less horrified. At first my ears don't even quite know how to process what they're hearing. "It's in the Catskills," my mother continues, "and you can ride horses."

"Horses?" I repeat uncomprehendingly and have to steady myself on a chair back as my knees start to buckle.

"They have all kinds of activities. Three-legged races, cookouts, canoeing . . ." Each word more hideous than the one preceding it. "Yes, tell me more about how my life is going to end." I think at this point I depart my body and float above the room, looking down on the now empty shell of my nine-year-old self with complete detachment. "How peaceful he looks."

My parents, while trying to entice me with their idea of a child's idyllic summer had instead conjured a hellscape worse than anything Dante could have imagined. If we had smelling salts this would have been the perfect opportunity to use them.

I'm sure from my reaction they had an indication that this was not going to go their way. Finally, my mother says, "Well you can't just stay home all summer!"

"WHY NOT?!"

The really perverse thing was that my sister, Maria, who was three grades older than me, had always dreamed of going to sleepaway camp. This was something we'd only ever seen in movies; as far as we were concerned sleepaway camp was something just for rich kids. But unfortunately for Maria, the offer was only good for me. They were only going to spend that money if it was going to get a head case like myself out of the house. They weren't going to waste it on my sister, who was already happy as a pig in shit going to Clearview Day Camp. I remember her looking at the brochure longingly, saying, "It's not fair!"

Neither is having to grow up gay in Queens, Maria!

Shortly after, they relent. "Fine. Go downstairs and

watch TV," my father says defeated. "Thanks," I respond, already halfway there. "I'll see you in September."

And that is where I spend every day that summer. In front of the TV. My sofa, my cat, potato chips, Coke. Sunlight creeping through the small basement windows. If I could tape them with cardboard I would.

It is the same summer that New York City is terrorized by Son of Sam, the serial killer who is given orders by a Labrador retriever. Each day a new headline jumps from the *Daily News*. He communicates solely with one of the paper's chief reporters. The city is transfixed. It's the first time I've ever heard of a serial killer before and I'm not going to lie, it adds a certain *je ne sais quoi* to life in Flushing. It is also the summer where we experience a sweltering heat wave and a two-day citywide blackout. (Even at nine I was like, "This is A LOT.")

I watched any and everything on TV. And liked most all of it. Although I despised both *One Day at a Time* and *Alice*, I never missed an episode of either. Already hate watching before it was in vogue. Criticizing each show relentlessly for their entire runs. Now I look back on them with the same fondness you have for a long dead relative whose faults you've conveniently forgotten.

Each night looking forward to the prime-time line-ups. *Happy Days* on Tuesday, *Charlie's Angels* on Wednesday. But there was no night for TV like Saturday night. Because this was the night *The Carol Burnett Show* was on.

*The Carol Burnett Show* was a variety show. Sketches, music, guest stars. But mostly it was just Carol, and each week she would answer questions from the audience and I would dream that I was in that audience instead of where I was. I would start getting excited for the show on Wednesday. By Friday I couldn't eat. Saturday it was the only thought in my head. In that week's *TV Guide* I could find out what sketches she'd be performing, who the guest was going to be, each word sending me into spasms of joy. There was nobody like Carol. I loved her.

And the twisted thing was that I wasn't even allowed to stay up to see the show most weeks. It was on at 10:00 P.M., which was my bedtime. Once in a while there was a special episode that was on earlier. And every so often my mother would let me stay up to see it, so worn down was she from the constant pleading that I usually started days in advance. But she was capricious, my mother. Some weeks I'd ask once and she'd say okay. Others it was no, and there was nothing I could do to change her mind. In fact, the more I begged, the more resolved she became.

And on this night, this summer, when I am nine, I see in the *TV Guide* that Carol Burnett is doing a Eunice, Ed, and Mamma sketch, and I'm desperate to stay up late. Eunice, Ed, and Mamma was my absolute favorite. Like a perfect little play inside of the show, occasionally with its own commercial break in the middle, giving me even longer to savor it. Sometimes an hour could hold so much.

But this night, this summer, when I am nine, my mother says no. And not any amount of bargaining or cajoling will change her mind. It's almost impressive what she can withstand. How little I can move her. I see that this is going to be one of the weeks where I have lost. And I hate to lose. Lying in bed, wide awake. Sweating in the heat. (My parents having refused to put the air-conditioning on because we had it on yesterday. The logic to this is lost on me. Were we only allowed comfort on odd-numbered days? Put it on every day! Let's live like kings!) Besides, who the fuck could sleep knowing Carol was right there? So close. Happiness an on/off switch away.

(Many years later, when I am writing for television in Los Angeles, I meet Carol Burnett at a charity event. She is with a writer I know, and they stop briefly to say hello. Inside I am buzzing, the room now only me and Carol. Carol and me. How do you tell someone that they were your childhood? That some weeks they saved you? That because of them, you would imagine new endings to the sketches you loved most, new jokes—that you started writing in your head without even knowing that's what it was you were doing, only to realize it decades later. That without them you might not have ever even become a writer. Might not be standing here right now, in this very spot, in front of them. How do you tell someone that? You don't.)

And now, in bed, sweating, sweating, I hear a noise that I've never heard before. It sounds like a helicopter. And it is. And now there are lights flooding through our windows. And the doorbell rings. At 10:00 P.M.! Which is something that had never happened before. And I get out of bed and I look to see who it is. Creeping in my pajamas. The gay child already sniffing out drama like a bloodhound. A policeman is standing at our front door talking to my mother. I've never seen a policeman on our block before, much less at our door. The squad car out front, lights blinking. And now the most extraordinary thing happens. They think Son of Sam might be in our neighborhood. Might be in someone's yard. They want us to stay inside. Helicopters scanning the entire street. A serial killer! In *our* backyard! It was all too wonderful!

My mother lets me stay up, in the sudden excitement all bets are off, and I sit in front of the TV (windows now locked, cool air-conditioning filling the room) watching Eunice, Ed, and Mamma as policemen comb through our backyard with flashlights. Thinking life doesn't get much better than this.

It ended up being a false alarm and Son of Sam (also known as the .44 Caliber Killer—you know you're doing something right as a serial killer when they give you *two* names) continues his murderous rampage for several months more until he is finally caught. Now I'm not saying he wasn't a vicious monster, but I am saying he did do me a small favor one summer night, when the city was on fire.

# Teaching
# Little Fingers
# How to Play

I START TAKING PIANO LESSONS IN THE THIRD GRADE. My mother insists both my sister and I learn an instrument. Maria, since she is older, starts learning first. Then I follow three years later. Maria takes to it right away. She practices every afternoon and advances steadily. Forced to entertain company on holidays with a concert of Bach or Beethoven on our upright.

I take lessons on Wednesday afternoons at The

Church on the Hill. (I went to Catholic school. We only had a half day of school on Wednesdays so the kids who went to public school could come on Wednesday afternoons to take religion classes. To this day it feels weird to do any work past noon on a Wednesday.) The Church on the Hill was a Protestant church in the neighborhood where my piano teacher had his office and gave lessons. The Church on the Hill was a no-frills, nondescript building. (If you're going to build a church, take a page from the Catholics and fucking *build it*. The Catholics are the *RuPaul's Drag Race* of religions. We put on a show, honey.) The Church on the Hill was the kind of place where they had AA meetings on Tuesday nights. St. Mel's did not have AA meetings. That was some kind of liberal bullshit. In the '70s Catholics didn't even use the word *alcoholic*, we just said Irish.

My piano teacher, Mr. Anderson, was the first adult male that I knew who rode a bicycle. This was, no doubt, another sign of the freewheeling Protestant lifestyle. Each Wednesday I might as well have been going to Woodstock. My first music book was titled *Teaching Little Fingers How to Play*, after that, things would get increasingly more challenging. And if little fingers don't practice, little fingers don't learn how to play. I was able to muddle my way through the first year on my scant charm and the simplicity of the early material. Much like learning another language, it's from year two on where you're really fucked. Any idiot can memorize a few vocabulary words, but I still don't know what the past imperfect is, nor do I ever wish to find out. I've made it this far.

Mr. Anderson insisted I practice every day after school in order to improve. He actually could get pretty pissy for a Protestant youth minister or whatever else he did outside of teaching piano and adult bike riding. By the time I had been taking lessons for about two years or so my sister had already advanced beyond what Mr. Anderson was capable of teaching her and had been sent to study on Saturdays at the Manhattan School of Music. (Her concerts for company now accompanied with a prologue from my mother about her advanced studies. I was often entreated to be her opening act, but, darling, even at ten, I was nobody's opening act, "no thank you, I'll just sit here listening for mistakes.")

I, on the other hand, still apparently had years more to learn from Mr. Anderson. It's not that I didn't want to practice, it's more that I never got around to it. My TV watching schedule was intense and allowed little room for flexibility. Plus you don't have to practice on Wednesday, that's the day you have the lesson. And Thursday is super close to Wednesday, you still have an eternity before your next lesson. Friday is the best day of the week, so don't waste it on practicing. Saturday, see Friday. Sunday is spent in a crippling depression. How can any human being focus on scales when the horrors of a fresh week are ticking down? By Monday, well, I really do have to practice. But then realize how far behind I am, and it's all suddenly too much. Tuesday is better spent plotting excuses than actually practicing, which by this time is way too late anyway. As if school wasn't a torture enough, I now also had this once-weekly added terror to contend with. It was like being told by a doctor that you had cancer and your cancer also had cancer. The drive to The Church on the Hill Wednesday afternoons became its own mini-torment. There was one traffic light on the way to that church, and I swear to God for the ten years I took lessons it was always green. I would pray for the light to turn red as we were approaching it, if only to buy myself a few more moments of freedom before the inevitable. But it was like we were in the Indy 500 when we were going to that fucking church. It was a straight shot to hell.

My excuses for not practicing would vary from: the books fell behind the piano and I couldn't find them, to the garden variety of children's illnesses, to the stubborn insistence that I *did* practice and I have no idea what's happening now. "I did it right at home!" But to fuck things up even further, some rare weeks I *would* practice, and on those weeks my lesson went well. Mr. Anderson now coming to life. Maybe I *will* play for the company next time, Maria. You can sit this one out, dear. Also, I liked keeping Mr. Anderson off-balance. Just when you've written me off . . . here comes little Liberace. (Even as a closeted gay boy I instinctively knew that keeping people off-balance was a tool that would come in handy in life. This must also be part of the DNA makeup that determines sexuality.)

At any given time, I usually had one exercise book (hated), two classical books (hated), and after a few years of lessons, a Broadway sheet music book (LOVED). These I *would* practice. Learning the score to *West Side Story* and *Brigadoon* and *Cabaret*. I'll pass on the Bach concertos, Mr. Anderson, and take a double helping of "A Boy Like That." After I finished learning the score to one Broadway musical, I would immediately start another. When I'm twelve years old the next book I get is for the musical *The Best Little Whorehouse in Texas* and I'm obsessed with everything in it. Now, at the time it didn't seem unusual to me that my piano teacher, who was also a Protestant youth minister (I think), would assign me the sheet music to *The Best Little Whorehouse in Texas.* And my mother certainly didn't seem to think there was anything unusual with me belting out *"Texas has a whorehouse in it / Lord have mercy on our souls!"* for a half hour each night.

"Sounding good!" she'd call from upstairs while preparing dinner. (If the cat ran across the keyboard, she'd still say "sounding good," so I took her compliments with a grain of salt.) But my favorite song was "Hard Candy Christmas" and I'd play it over and over. In this song the hookers have to leave the whorehouse because it's closing and they dream about their life outside the whorehouse walls. And I sang it constantly. (For full effect please Google the Original Broadway Cast recording of this song and listen to it now.)

*Hey, maybe I'll learn to sew / Maybe I'll just lie low / Maybe I'll hit the bars / Maybe I'll count the stars until the dawn / Me, I will go on.*

Now typically a song about women who had been sexually exploited by dozens of men and faced an uncertain future after a lifetime of abuse wouldn't be the obvious choice for a twelve-year-old boy. But what can I say? Their pain was my pain.

I continue my piano lessons a few years longer. But my heart's no longer in it (was it ever?).

(My sister, on the other hand, by this time is a piano performance major at NYU. And she actually has a part-time job playing at a French restaurant on Long Island. We go see her one night at La Bibliothèque, my parents and I. Have dinner as she plays in the cocktail lounge. Me scraping the gloppy sauce off of the entrée I hate. (Italians only like Italian restaurants, I learn this at a very young age. This was the first time I think my parents had ever taken me to a French restaurant. The countries are right next door to each other, I have no idea why French food seemed so much more frighteningly sophisticated. Like you needed to go to college to eat it.) Maria was all of eighteen years old, if she had been performing at Carnegie Hall it couldn't have been more thrilling.)

I finally tell my mother I want to stop my lessons. And she says that I can. But if I do stop I have to take up another activity, sport, or instrument, or basically any fucking thing. She's clever my mother, I'll give her that. Since I have never done one extracurricular activity, I certainly don't plan to start now. So I continue with my lessons at The Church on the Hill. Every Wednesday afternoon praying for the one traffic light to turn red that never does. And by now Mr. Anderson and I are like an old married couple. He knows all my tricks and we don't have to pretend any longer. What did I practice, let's just work on that, cut to the chase. His bicycle still in the room. A comfort at this point. If this is my only option then I will come up this hill until I die. (Which is even a Protestant-sized hill. Not too large or too small, nothing that would offend.)

Now I don't want to say I have no friends in high school, but they are few and far between. They're not even friends, more acquaintances, really. Like people who work on another floor of your office building that you ride the elevator with each day. "Morning," then back to staring at the buttons.

I spend most of my time avoiding people. Trying to blend in. Hoping not to be noticed. But there is this one boy, Jim. And he is tall and handsome and straight and has the effortless confidence of all boys who are tall and handsome and straight. I think we are in a class together, maybe. And he is friendly to me. And that's enough for me to fixate on him, enough for me to imagine us as friends. No, there is no part of me that thinks he is gay, or in any way wants anything from him other than friendship (I think). But this is not a skill that I have acquired. Making friends. I observe other boys talking

to each other with the same kind of bemused detachment I would two monkeys at the zoo. Fascinating, but
no takeaways that would apply to my actual life. Spending all your time avoiding subjects—sports, girls, cars—
gives you scant conversational solid ground. I was always
scrambling for any overlapping topics whenever Jim and
I were thrown together. Once a teacher died, so that was
super helpful. I dined out on that for a few weeks. What
kid doesn't want to talk about a dead teacher?

I think Jim is a stoner, which would explain his
constant dopey, affable demeanor. Big white teeth, easy
smile, good hair. We now say "hi" maybe three days a
week and it's the most intense friendship in my life. I
nurture it delicately like a sickly plant with one tiny
flower. We are both sophomores at St. Francis Prep.
Both fifteen. And I'm trying to figure out how we can
further cement our friendship. Conversation has dried
up as of late, and short of killing another teacher I'm
going to have to do something radical to help take our
relationship to the next level. Winter break is approaching and I ask Jim for his phone number. Ask him maybe
if he wants to do something over break. He says "sure."
I have never done anything like this before in my life.
It feels momentous. Like buying a house. He rips off

a piece of notebook paper, scribbles his number, and that's that. I am aware of where that paper is every second of the day.

And shortly thereafter, winter break comes and I go into my father's office in our basement. It is in the back, unfinished part with the washer and dryer and Ping-Pong table. The only place in our house that can be considered private, and I take out that piece of paper and I try to summon the courage to call him. Calling a friend in the '80s was a fucking nightmare. Of course today you would be able to text each other and the whole thing wouldn't have taken on the dramatic heft of, say, the Nuremberg trials. And not only did you have to deal with the stress of talking to the person you were calling, but you also had the added stress of dealing with whoever answered the fucking phone. A sibling, mother, or God forbid, a father (this was rare). First, you'd identify yourself. "Hi, Mrs. blank, is blank home, this is Gary from school." Then you'd have to wait while said child is called for and then you'd have to hear the child's bewilderment when he finds out who is on the other end of the phone. "What? Who?" The whole thing is a sickening smorgasbord of humiliations that thankfully this generation has been spared.

And then I do something so strange that it haunts me to this day. My stomach still churning at the memory.

"Hi, is Jim home, this is Gary from school."

"Hold on please. Jim!" Moments later.

"Hello?"

"Hey, Jim, I was wondering if you wanted to go to the half-price ticket booth with me tomorrow to get tickets to the matinee of *The Best Little Whorehouse in Texas*."

"Uh, no, thanks."

"Okay, well bye."

And I hang up the phone and sit there at my father's desk (littered with cruise brochures for his job with Cunard Line) frozen. I don't know exactly why what I did was so wrong, but from his response I instantly know that this is not something that fifteen-year-old boys normally do together (wishing myself into the photo facing me of a happy honeymoon couple playing shuffleboard).

I see Jim in school the following week. He is as friendly as he always has been. But I can't look at him. All I can do is imagine what he said to his mother after he hung up the phone and she asked what did he want, and Jim has to then say to his mother, "He asked if I wanted to go to a matinee of *The Best Little Whorehouse in Texas*." "What?" she'd ask. "You heard me," he'd respond. (Today, of course, there are millions of young boys, little Dear Evan Hansens everywhere, who would die to go to a Broadway matinee. Not then. There were no chat rooms. No social media. No way to find my people. Then there was just me. The only boy at St. Francis Prep who spent the Wednesday of his winter break freezing in line for one discount ticket to *The Best Little Whorehouse in Texas*.) The sickly plant that I'd been nurturing already dead. I feel stupid. Imagining a friendship that never was. Will never be. He's just a nice kid saying hello to someone in his class, nothing more. And I grabbed on to something as simple as that until I strangled the life out of it.

I finally do stop taking piano lessons. I think at the end of my junior year. It's clear nothing is going to change at this point. I have never stayed once at school even five minutes past the final bell. I have never gone to anyone's house to watch TV. Gone out on the weekend to a party. Joined a club. Thrown a ball. When I say again I want to stop lessons, this time my mother just says "okay." No bargains left to be made. I'm seventeen, probably. Mr. Anderson and I mostly talk during my last lesson. He tells me about a bicycle trip he will be going on. I think I play one or two pieces before we say goodbye. My mother comes to pick me up. She doesn't ask me what I will do now. What I will join, what sport I will play. Nothing. We drive home in silence. I have both won something and lost.

*I'll be fine and dandy / Lord it's like a hard candy Christmas / I'm barely getting through tomorrow / But still I won't let / Sorrow bring me way down.*

# J's

IT'S 1992, I'M IN MY EARLY TWENTIES (OKAY MID-twenties), and there's this kind of club near where I live in the Village. I walk by it all the time. It's at the edge of the Meatpacking District. You know how when you catch an episode from an early season of *The Real Housewives* and see how different their original faces were? That's what the Meatpacking District was like then. No Soho House or Gansevoort Hotel or Apple

Store or Starbucks Reserve. Just Florent, a French bistro open twenty-four hours a day that everyone went to and was fabulous in a way that nothing is anymore, a few leather bars, a bagel place, and actual meatpacking plants. And J's Hangout.

J's Hangout was as seedy as a club could be, and I had never been inside. It was not a sex club per se. It was more of a bar where the guys at some point in the evening all stood around and jerked off in front of each other. Usually in a circle. So, yeah, a bar where guys got into a circle jerk every night. I won't lie, I was curious. I was never in a fraternity in college but I assumed that it was pretty much that. At this point in my young life I consider myself a writer (even though I don't actually write), and anything I do I chalk up to "research." For what, I don't know, but research allows you to do a lot of things you wouldn't normally do if, say, you weren't a writer (which I'm technically not) doing research.

I never have the courage to go in, though. Truth be told I was not a sex club kind of person. I was more of a "let's go see *The Princess Bride* and then you can walk me home and maybe I'll show you my wrist" kind of person. A cocktease, if you must. I wanted to be romanced. Pursued. I don't know where I got this idea, I'd never seen it in actual life. Yes, I wanted sex but more than that I wanted someone who would take me out to a fuck-ing restaurant. If I could go back to 1992 I'd slap twenty-five-year-old Gary across the face hard and tell him to knock it off. But twenty-five-year-old Gary wanted to fall in love. He wanted to be swept off his feet. He wanted flowers. He wanted theater tickets. He wanted it all.

I'd moved to the city from Queens to go to graduate school at NYU but never finished. I wanted to write, but since I wasn't writing in school, I figured I could just as well get a job and not write and save some money on tuition. I move to an apartment on the sixth floor of a walk-up on Christopher Street. The kind of place where the bathroom has no sink and the other tenants have lived there over fifty years. In a movie it would be charming. In real life it was just disgusting.

My gym, only a few blocks away. Your gym even more important than your apartment. There's a boy there I like. I arrange my workouts to overlap with his. Imag-ining he's my boyfriend and we just happen to be work-ing out on opposite ends of the gym floor but will go home together and cook dinner and watch TV and he is mine. I observe every detail about him. "He's growing his hair out"; "I've never seen that watch before"; "He hasn't worn those shorts in a while." Tall and muscular and quiet with sandy hair, I've already got us picking out mattresses and we've never even said "hello." On days he's not there I deflate. Spending my workout wondering where he is, what he's doing, who he's with. Then, the next time he reappears, I'm aloof. *Oh, look who's decided to come waltzing back*, I think, clocking his every move. Watching him go through his workout unaware of the fight we're having in my head. Only to be quickly forgiven the second he does something adorable, like wipe the sweat from his upper lip with the bottom of his T-shirt, revealing his perfect stomach. God, I fucking love him.

It wasn't as easy to meet guys then as it is now, swiping through people like paint chips. In the '90s we didn't have Grindr, we had phone sex. Which was way less efficient and much more expensive. The phone bill an airline ticket to Europe each month. Some months Australia. And to add insult to injury I wasn't even very good at it.

The numbers were advertised in all the free little magazines you'd get in bars—there was this one called *HX* (Homo Extra it stood for I believe, this passed for cleverness in the '90s, take that Oscar Wilde) that was basically the gay bible. It had all the bars in the five boroughs, which night was which club, bookstores, restaurants, everything a gay person could possibly need to know. And it came out every week. Thursdays. I don't know how I still remember this. I couldn't tell you the plot of *A Tale of Two Cities* which I read last month, but *HX* magazine is still burned into my brain. And it had a section that I liked to think of as the society pages, where all the A-gays were photographed shirtless at the clubs and, in some cases, suited at charity events. I had never been to a charity event except as a cater waiter, and these men in these photos might as well have been Bette Davis and Joan Fontaine in *Photoplay* magazine. I couldn't imagine having my picture in *HX*.

Sometimes I'd see these men out at the clubs and the bars and recognize them from the glossy pages and be too shy to approach them. These are *HX* magazine stars, gay royalty, I don't travel in their circles. Summer shares in the Pines, brunches, dinner parties. Lives only to be glimpsed briefly once a week as I pick up my new issue, leaf through the pages, pausing at the perfect torsos, and then stuff into my pocket, to later bring back to my apartment to replace last week's copy. If there was a gay apartment that didn't have *HX* magazine in it, I'd never been inside.

The phone sex line was also relentlessly advertised on *The Robin Byrd Show*, a public access program that was basically *The Tonight Show* if *The Tonight Show* were hosted by a former porn star who, at the end of each episode, had her guests get naked and then pretended to poke her eye out with their genitalia. It was strangely much more wholesome than it sounds. With a Mickey and Judy "let's put on a show" kind of pluck that you just don't find anymore.

The way it worked was this, you called some 1–800 number and you'd get connected to someone in your area who would immediately ask your dick size. I preferred a bit of chitchat first. "Are you reading anything good?" "Where was your last vacation?" Click and I'd be on to the next caller. I was desperate to find *one* person with a sense of humor. Or who would at least answer one question that didn't involve either the word top or bottom. I guess you don't call a phone sex line for the witty banter.

I called so often I started recognizing the voices. "You wanna suck my big cock?" Oh, her again. "No thank you, dear." Next caller, please. Occasionally, I could keep someone on the phone for a few minutes, just chatting about nothing much. A tiny connection. Our dull conversation at least twenty dollars. (Was I the sad john from every movie who goes to the hooker just to talk?) We didn't give our phone number freely then. Now you give it more easily than a smile, but in the '90s we protected them like the nuclear codes. I have no idea why.

But the thought that I'd give my number to someone on the phone sex line was as unimaginable as giving them my house keys. It just wasn't done.

What's funny is I don't even remember ever having had actual phone sex. I'm sure I must have, it was pretty much another rent's worth of calls a month. I do remember saying "I'm never going to call that again," after hanging up a lot. What I was looking for I'm not sure. Something. Anything.

I did hook up once with a man I'd met on the phone sex line (for some reason a home address was given more freely than a number). I showed up at his apartment, heart beating out of my chest, "research" I repeat like a mantra, waiting for the door to open, and when it does he's gorgeous and my first thought is, I should have been doing this ages ago. And the apartment is nice. Real furniture. A dining room. Art. *HX* magazine on the table. What was more wondrous than a gay upper-middle-class apartment? We start kissing and our clothes are off and I feel freer than I have ever felt in my life, until we hear a key in the door and he jumps off me like a cartoon cat and yells "Quick, hide!" shoving me naked into the bathroom. I listen to his older boyfriend enter the apartment and the subsequent unraveling of their relationship. The younger boyfriend folding like a house of cards when the older one instantly notices something is amiss. "He's in the bathroom!"

Apparently older boyfriend has come home early from a business trip (managing to be at once both glamorous and hackneyed) and I'm relegated to the role of "some random slut" as older boyfriend refers to me. A part I secretly like since it's not one I'd ever cast myself in. "How dare he?" I whisper offended to no one as I crouch naked on their toilet seat. There's no way I can exit this bathroom without my clothes and it's not like anyone had a cell phone then. I can't even remember my life without a phone. How vulnerable we all were all the time. Out in the world alone. Anything could happen. And it just did! I'd been in this apartment no more than five minutes before all hell broke loose. It's not fair. How long will I have to stay in here? Will the older boyfriend come in and kill me? Fortunately, gay men usually don't commit crimes of passion, they're more likely to just join in. I suddenly hear the young boyfriend start crying. From what I can glean through the door this has happened many times before. "*He's* the slut!" I say, again to no one. A few more minutes go by until silence and then the young boyfriend knocks lightly on the door. Which seems overly polite, considering our circumstances. I open it a crack and he hands me my clothes and says "sorry" and I say "oh, no, that's okay," as if this happens to me all the time. "Would you mind hurrying up?" "No, I'd like to spend as long as possible in here."

A second later I'm fully dressed and now have to walk through the apartment as the older boyfriend sits on the sofa glaring at me. The length of the room expanding endlessly like the hallway in *Poltergeist*. My first walk of shame and I didn't even get to do the fun part, just a disproportionate amount of the shame part. The younger boyfriend walks me the final way to the door, which I appreciate. In my mind I'm now pretending I only stopped by to visit this couple for a drink, not to put the final nail in the coffin of their relationship. Erasing the humiliation of the evening with each step that takes me closer to freedom. "This didn't happen, this didn't happen."

I never meet anyone again through the phone sex line. I meet guys mostly at the gym, I guess, the hotel where I work as a bellman, sometimes there. But never anyone that I cook dinner with, never anyone whose arms I fall asleep in and wake up in. Never that.

One night, one day, one summer, I'm walking past J's Hangout. (Or am I *not* walking past it, like a murder—is it premeditated, did I *know* I was going in there from the very first time I heard about it? "Circle jerks, you say? In a bar?" Files away for later.)

And now I'm there. At the door. In shorts and an NYU tank top. And I go in. More "research." And it's thrilling and gross in equal measure (most truly thrilling things are). It's an open space, not as dimly lit as you would expect, and the term no-frills would be an understatement. If sticky could be a room, it would be this. There are several men standing at the bar, a few walking around, and then toward the back (I mean barely toward the back, like a few feet away) guys stand in a circle jerking off. I saunter around with my beer (I don't drink beer, I never know what to order) like it's the most natural thing on earth. How provincial one would have to be to think that this was in any way unusual. I play it cool. Glancing over at the circle as if it's a conversation I'm considering joining, maybe later. Truth be told I'm not certain of the proper etiquette at a circle jerk bar. I don't want to stare and yet I'm not sure if it's something you just join in on, or, not unlike a deli counter, take a number and wait your turn.

As I'm doing a lap of the room, I see him. My gym boyfriend. He stands alone, nursing a drink. My first thought is shame, I don't want him to see me here, but then I realize he's here, too. I walk by him and we catch eyes. He smiles at me, I smile back and make a face that implies I'm trying to figure out where I know him from. He says, "The gym, right?" and I say something like, "Oh, my God, of course, hi, nice to see you," and suddenly it's like being at an office holiday party except the floor is covered in ejaculate.

"So what do you do?" I say, pretending men aren't orgasming three feet away from us. That this is any normal "meet cute." A story to tell our friends and eventually our children.

And even though we are standing in a bar I ask him if he'd like to go out for a drink sometime. He says, "Sure," and we exchange numbers (this is a circumstance where you *do* give your number out). And I wish we could've met anyplace else. And then he says, "Well, it was nice seeing you."

"Oh, God, so nice seeing you, too. I'll call you."

"I'd like that," he says. And I'm thinking, Well, I can't join the circle jerk NOW! THAT can't be our first date! We haven't even kissed! But he's not leaving. So I say good night and I walk home. Grabbing the new *HX* from the open doorway of a bar as I go by.

# The Wizard of Oz

WHEN I FIRST SAW *THE WIZARD OF OZ* I WAS three. And I can still remember watching it that first time and thinking, Oh fuck yes, this is for me. The third or fourth time I saw it we had a new television set, and when Dorothy went to Oz and the screen suddenly turned color, I lost my shit. If my mother had taken a giant dump on the living room carpet right in front of me I would've shown less surprise. "IT'S IN COLOR?!

WHAT THE FUCK?!" I always eyed my parents suspiciously after that. What kind of a lunatic lets their child watch *The Wizard of Oz* on a black-and-white TV set without at least mentioning, "This part's supposed to be in color," when they get to Oz. But to spring it on us out of nowhere? I always waited for the other shoe to drop in any other movie that I watched after that, but this was, to my knowledge, the only film whose entire plot hinged on such a mind fuck.

It aired once a year on, or around, Easter. I sat mesmerized in front of the TV as if I were watching the moon landing. I looked forward to it the way a woman approaching forty would her wedding day. Christmas had nothing on the night *The Wizard of Oz* aired. I'm not going to go on about how much more special things were then, when you could only see them with the infrequency of, say, a dental exam, and had to delay gratification—the whole country watching as one, shared experiences, etcetera, etcetera. Pass. I would've much preferred to have been able to watch it at my whim, the way children watch things today. Tiny tyrants all of them, demanding to see their favorite movies over and over and over again until their parents are ready to blow their brains out. One mistimed bathroom break then, and just like that you'd have to wait another year to see Dorothy collapse from poppy dust. Do you know how hard it is to learn every line of a movie when you see it only once a year? Kids then had to WORK. No rewinding, no play it again. You had to wait an entire motherfucking year just to be certain the line was "you've always had the power, my dear, you just had to learn it for yourself." Glinda could've told Dorothy this a lot sooner, but then there would've been no movie, I guess. Dorothy goes home just by clicking her heels three times, but I never understood why she wanted to return so badly. Oz was fabulous. It was in color, for fuck's sake.

"I would've stayed," I think while watching every time. "I would've stayed forever."

"IT'S STARTING!" I would scream to my sister on those annual Sunday nights. (My idea of hell is reliving that Sunday night on a loop the second after *The Wizard of Oz* has ended. The total sickness I felt I can still summon.) You don't really have to scream "It's starting!" anymore to anyone ever about anything. All of life is paused until we're ready for it now. That's nice in its own way. Then the world didn't stop for anyone. If you wanted to watch *The Wizard of Oz* you better sit the fuck in front of the TV NOW or else you were going to have to wait another YEAR. Think of how barbaric that sounds today. And yet "IT'S STARTING!" still gives me a thrill. Like happening upon your favorite song while flipping through radio stations in the car, the song always sounds so much better somehow than when you put it on yourself.

It's funny how *The Wizard of Oz* never seems like an old movie. Never dates, never goes out of style. It's of its own time. Or maybe it just seems that way to me. When I was a kid I obviously didn't know it was the gayest motion picture ever made. (Or did I?) And if anybody is reading this thinking, It is? Yes, dear, it is. Dorothy is the quintessential fag hag. She hangs out with three gay men. THEY'RE GAY! (Jesus. Come on. They perform musical numbers.) Also the black-and-white-to-color thing is like the gayest thing ever. The movie is literally one big drag reveal. Then there's the Wicked Witch of the West, perhaps the best villain in all of film history. Villains don't need to have backstories, by the way. She's a fucking bitch, I don't need to know how she got like that. All she has to do is scare me. And Margaret Hamilton scared the shit out of me. But I couldn't look away from her. Is there any moment more chilling than when Dorothy is desperate to get home and she is a prisoner of the witch and cries for Aunty Em, and then Aunty Em appears in the globe and Dorothy is going into hysterics because Aunty Em can't see her and she breaks down sobbing,

"Aunty Em, Aunty Em, I'm right here!" and then the Wicked Witch appears, mocking her, "Aunty Em, Aunty Em!" and then laughs at her. She fucking laughs at her. I still lose my mind when I see that part. It's so vicious. And I love it. The Wicked Witch never makes any stupid jokes like she would now. Or has a song. Or ever has a moment when she hesitates about what she's doing. "Is there a way to get the slippers back *without* killing Dorothy?" She doesn't have a vulnerable moment like Meryl Streep has in *The Devil Wears Prada*. (Which I feel like was way more human than Anna Wintour is in real life anyway, so why put it in?) No, thank you. Margaret Hamilton played it as if this wasn't for kids. She wasn't soft-pedaling it for us. You could either take it or you couldn't. She didn't give a fuck.

And another thing that makes it so super gay? Dorothy is looking for something better, someplace she belongs, somewhere over the rainbow (which the studio wanted to cut from the movie for "slowing it down." Can you fucking believe that? It still pisses me off). And aren't all gay people looking for someplace we can call our own? Where we will be safe. Loved.

But it wasn't any of those things that made it the most gay film of all time. It was Judy. At only sixteen years old she already knows real pain. The kind of pain that most gay children can also identify with. She is damaged. So young. And when she sings about going over the rainbow she is crying. She is broken. And it's haunting. Because it is real. And you say "Yes, I want to go, too. Let me go with you." You recognize yourself in her. You recognize her pain. Two lost, broken things calling out to each other through the screen. This is no children's performance, no G-rated pablum. This is raw fucking hurt. This is someone who knows us, who sees us. And, yes, she travels over the rainbow and wears ruby slippers, and kills *two* witches and gets her hair blown out and sings and there are Munchkins and flying monkeys. (No amount of CGI, by the way, could create anything nearly as terrifying. CGI has no soul. Something needs to have a soul in order for it to be truly frightening.) But none of these are the reasons *The Wizard of Oz* has remained a gay touchstone for over eighty years. Judy Garland's pain is the reason. That we understand. That connects us forever. The rest is just icing on a very marvelous cake, the moments we can enjoy together without having to confront the darker thing just underneath.

All I ever wanted was to leave Queens. To go someplace where I wouldn't feel alone any longer. And I did. But now I come back. Often. And my parents are still in the same house I watched *The Wizard of Oz* in all those years ago. And when I visit, I walk up to the door, that door I have walked up to for over fifty years, and my mother is there to greet me. And she hugs me. "Gary's home," she calls to my father.

# Pen Pals

THIS WEIRD THING HAPPENED TO ME ONCE THAT I
had forgotten about until recently. I tucked it away
somewhere for years and suddenly, just like that, it
popped back up. I'm going to have to, unfortunately,
start at the beginning. I'll try to be brief.

My dad works for Cunard Cruise Line and we get to
go on free cruises. My parents, my sister, and me. One of
the perks of the job. This was before anyone even went

on cruises. Way before they were petri dishes for pandemics where you sailed around aimlessly for several weeks until you died. They were fun and civilized then. There were no drunken people falling off balconies only to be lost to the seas. No rock climbing walls or ten-story atriums. Ships looked like ships and people behaved like people.

We go on one, two a year. Usually to the Caribbean or Bermuda. But one year, when I'm fifteen, we get bumped off our cruise by Cunard Line days before we're supposed to set sail. (As an employee we were always subject to the possibility of a last-minute ejection, but this was the first time it had ever happened.) I was bereft. It literally felt like someone was taking the Oscar out of my hands. My father, feeling badly, finagles us onto another trip on Costa Cruises. (This is the line that becomes famous when years later one of their ships sinks off the coast of Italy and the captain is one of the first to leave the ship. Which, if you know *one* thing about being a captain, it's that that is the opposite of what's supposed to happen. My first thought when I see this on the news is "We went on a Costa Cruise!" I would venture to say we had a better time.)

We depart from San Juan on the *Carla C* for a week in the Caribbean. The *Carla C* is an old ship. The decks sagging in the middle, it's like walking across a piece of plywood atop two paint cans. The ship even has its own theme song that the waiters force us to sing each night at dinner. Since this is an Italian cruise line there is a lot of mediocre pasta on the menu. The nice thing about pasta on an Italian line is it can only be so bad. (I much prefer Cunard Line, the British cruise line my father works for, truth be told. Give me a British ship's officer over an Italian one any day of the week. Polite, sleek, blond men without arm hair thick enough to cut through their uniform sleeves. They don't age well, sadly, but nobody looks better than a British officer at twenty. By thirty they look as though they've spent the last decade on a rock in the middle of the ocean. Weather-beaten with six dull yellow hairs left, skin several different shades of red that should only be seen in before photos at a dermatologist's office, bloated from alcohol and almost toothless, their glory days already long behind them. But a Brit at twenty in a uniform? Well, there's nothing more beautiful.)

My sister and I quickly make friends with whatever other teenagers are on board. At home I have no friends. The other teenagers in school I would never think to be so chummy with. But here, on the open sea, the old rules don't apply. And the me that lives in Queens, well, nobody knows him. Being thrown together in these circumstances makes for quick easy friendships with the life span of a banana. Good for five, six days and then you toss it away. No emails to exchange, no phone numbers or Instagrams. No way of us knowing what each other's lives are like outside the confines of the ship. There is no before and there is no after. And teenagers on vacation, as a whole, are much less cruel. Occasionally my sister, Maria, and I exchange addresses with the kids we meet on these cruises. Writing letters back and forth for several months, a year at most, before the novelty wears off and trying to re-create the excitement of the week we spent together becomes just another drudgery.

One cruise our luggage doesn't arrive, and Maria ends up wearing the clothes of another teenager from Michigan for the week. They write letters to each other for a while. Her name was Kristy, and now I realize that was a sweet kid who did that. Sometimes kids can be so thoughtful without even knowing it. Usually they're horrible, though. Anything otherwise is just a pleasant surprise.

On another cruise, when Maria is eighteen and I'm sixteen, we befriend some other teenagers from Queens and two young men from Atlanta, both twenty-four. Cute in the way young people are cute. I, of course, become instantly obsessed with the two young men. I exchange addresses, and when we get home I instantly write them an insane letter asking about colleges in Georgia. I'm ready to move to Atlanta in order to be near these men who I now saw as my friends and protectors. Kindly, one of them writes me back. (Can you believe it? Now of course, in retrospect, it's a bit odd that an adult man in Georgia is writing to a sixteen-year-old in Queens, but the world was simpler then.) He recommends colleges to me. I'm moving to Georgia, I decide. These are my friends. We will become roommates and I will get a job. This is my new life now. Every letter you put out into the world meant your life could change with the response. Thankfully, they never write back after receiving my even more insane second letter. I have a vague memory of it and really wouldn't be surprised if they'd turned it over to the FBI.

But here on the *Carl C*, on this cruise, I am fifteen and I make friends with a young married couple, Nancy and Jack. She is a teacher and he does something in business. They're in their late twenties, I think, and from Los Angeles (the most glamorous place a person could be from as far as I was concerned). Again, I'm not sure why they're hanging out with a fifteen-year-old but I was never drawn to people my own age. I was often told it was charming that I had an old soul. Now my soul matches my face, which is decidedly less charming.

I go to the shows on board with Nancy and Jack, play bingo with them, attend the midnight buffet (more pasta, we get it), even take a shore excursion. My sister joins us sometimes, I think even my mother. Mostly just me, though. I couldn't possibly tell you what we talked about. But I could always pull some nonsense out of my ass when talking with adults. I don't think I ever really behaved like a child, I had no one to do it with. But adults I knew, I watched them on TV for twelve hours a day. It was a much more exciting world to me. Who wanted to be my stupid age? Of course, now I would cut off my own ear to be fifteen again for a half hour, but that's one of God's sick little jokes, isn't it? (As George Bernard Shaw famously said, "Youth is wasted on the young." One of the better quotes about the horrors of aging. Whenever I meet someone in their twenties I immediately want to show them a photo of myself in *my* twenties so they know I, too, once had my skin wrapped taut around my face.)

When we get home from the cruise (To this day I can still hear the song the waiters sang on the *Carla C* buzzing in my head. An insipid tune has an incredibly long shelf life. Or, as Noël Coward also famously said:

"Strange how potent cheap music is." You really should have known both these quotes. Especially the first one.) I become pen pals with Nancy and Jack. Really, just Nancy. She was the one who I most liked. And she writes back diligently and frequently. And for the first time I have an actual pen pal. Letters going back and forth between us on almost a weekly basis. I can't imagine what I'm writing about, since the only thing I do is watch television. Probably that. And after a year we keep writing. And another year goes by. And another. And I feel like I know Nancy and she knows me. And our friendship grows over the years until I am suddenly twenty and Nancy and Jack have a new baby.

I'm a junior at Hofstra University on Long Island by now (I finally do have friends my own age. The trajectory of that usually goes — wanting older friends, wanting friends your own age, wanting younger friends, death), when I decide to take my first trip to LA to visit them.

Nancy and Jack live in Long Beach, which I discover is not a part of LA. If anybody tells you that it is, they are lying. Long Beach is to LA what Ohio is to New York City. Completely disconnected. I fly into LA and decide to spend the first few days in Venice, which from what I gather from *Three's Company* has a boardwalk that people roller-skate along.

Today you could stay in any number of cute hotels with trendy furniture and small plates of tapas and a mixologist with a beard behind the bar. I would love to be in my twenties and poor now. There are so many options. Most of them taking place on a roof. We didn't have roofs in the '80s. Everything was inside buildings, not on top of them. Now there's Soho House in DUMBO (which also didn't exist) that has an entire restaurant, nightclub, and pool on the roof. Just being outside on a roof, holding a drink, makes everything that much cooler. Hats off to the person who from the sidewalk pointed up and said, "Let's put bars and pools and restaurants up there." When I was in my twenties, roofs were only for water towers and drying laundry. Now you get to stay in a hotel that's cheap(ish) and cute that has good food and drinks with a roof deck and you can swipe on your phone to find someone to meet you on the roof and then fuck in your trendy, cheap(ish) room.

But then, if you were twenty and had no money, you stayed at a youth hostel. Which was as disgusting as it sounds. I stay in a room with bunk beds that I share with two backpackers from the Netherlands who kindly offer me from their creepy bag of nuts and dried twigs. I politely decline. The bathroom looks like something intended to hose down incoming prisoners rather than host Dutch students. Just drains and showerheads. With the right crowd, lighting, and director it could be an incredibly sexy scene. Unfortunately, real life rarely lives up to what we imagine and instead was just a badly tiled room of fungus and stink frequented by unattractive, naked Europeans. (I'm sure it had its good weeks; I was not there on one of them.)

My hopes of making a new friend are quickly dashed when the guy in the bunk above me lets out a fart so huge it turns the page of my book. I stroll the Venice boardwalk and it does not look at all like the opening montage from *Three's Company*. It is filled with large tourists and drug addicts and cheap souvenir shops. Not one cute person passes me on roller skates. With nothing else to do I walk out onto the nearby beach and lie in the sun for the next eight hours.

The following day, horrifically sunburned, I get a bus for Long Beach. So far I'm having a terrible time, and based on my two nights at the youth hostel and eight hours tanning, have decided that Los Angeles is an awful place. I thought it would be filled with shirtless young men on bicycles and surfboards, jogging and waving, one after the other, like bottles on an assembly line. I don't know where these guys were but they sure as hell weren't at the fucking Venice Youth Hostel. My *Playgirl* fantasy replaced by bland midwestern couples in spandex drinking from large, sticky cups.

Nancy and Jack pick me up at the bus station in Long Beach (perhaps the most depressing sentence I have ever written). I am excited to see them, Nancy especially. The equivalent of a pen pal today is being friends with someone on Instagram that you've never met. You feel you know them, but in reality it's like knowing a container of milk—you see it in your refrigerator several times a day but that doesn't mean you're friends.

I think I first know something is amiss from the moment they pick me up. You know how when you date someone and your first impression of them is, "I hate this person," but then you later think, "Oh, I was too hard on them, I actually like them," so you date them for a year only to realize your first impression *was* correct and you *do* hate them? That's kind of what this was like. My stomach dropped the instant I saw them. Something looked off, and my first thought was to flee, but I had nowhere to go. I couldn't pull my phone out of my pocket like you lucky sons of bitches. I told myself this was all in my head. Nancy hugs me so hard my back cracks. Not the kind of hug that says I missed you, more the kind of hug that says save me. They take me to their car where Nancy's mother-in-law waits for us, and I can tell instantly that she hates me. I have no idea why. She says hello to me in a manner that indicates she's on to me and whatever I was planning on trying won't work with her. We go directly to a restaurant that is not Applebee's but very much resembles Applebee's.

At dinner we catch up and I try to convince myself this is going to be fine. Everything's going to be just fine. You're too judgmental, I tell myself. (I actually wasn't judgmental then. I am now, though.) Nancy barely speaks. The mother-in-law glowers at me. Jack is perfectly friendly, seemingly oblivious to the tension at the table. Their one-year-old child is with us, sitting in his high chair. I desperately look to him for any clues on what the fuck is happening here, but he just drools uselessly. Oh, how I wish I were back at the youth hostel sharing a bag of muesli with Gijsbrecht and Oslop!

I try to engage Nancy in conversation. "How has teaching been?" She murmurs a noncommittal response while looking to her mother-in-law for approval. The large mother-in-law in the brightly colored clothing of a game show contestant, continues staring at me arms folded, as though she is waiting for a long overdue apology. Any sane person would've gotten themselves drunk by this point in the evening. But my mother has so ingrained in us the importance of being the perfect guest that I don't feel it is within my rights to say, "What the fuck is your problem, lady?" (As Italian-Americans, when I was a child my father grew tomatoes in our backyard. Every August we would have fresh tomato salads at dinner. Sliced tomatoes, olive oil, and salt. And when the tomatoes were finished we would dip our bread (Italian-Americans have bread at every meal) into the bowl and sop up all the remaining juice. When we were old enough to be invited to someone's house for dinner (I think I was only ever invited once, and it was with my sister), my mother, petrified that we would show up at this house and dip our bread in whatever tray or bowl of juice or sauce of any kind they had on the table, drums into our heads, "You are NEVER to do this outside of the house, do you understand me! NEVER! SWEAR!" You'd think we were biting off the heads of chickens at our kitchen table. This was something, my sister and I, of course, would have never thought to do at someone else's house. Ironically, though, after that, and for the rest of my life, whenever I'm at someone's house for dinner, it takes all of my self-restraint not to take a piece of bread, lean across the table, and dip it into the salad.)

When the bill comes the mother-in-law reaches into her purse and pulls out several coupons she hands to the waiter. All of their entrées are apparently free and I am left to pay for mine. She pays for their beverages with rolls of pennies and does not leave a tip for the waiter. How did this woman never come up in any of the letters Nancy writes to me?! It would be all I would be writing about day and night. "Guess who paid for her dinner with rolls of pennies again? I hate her sooo much!" And what were we writing about in these letters, anyway? I have no possible idea, clearly nothing with remotely any substance. Nothing more than cross-country cocktail party chitchat. Barely one conversation stretched out over the course of half a decade.

Later, back at their condo, which abuts a golf course, after we drop off the mother-in-law (byeeeeeee!), I turn in early. We have a big day tomorrow. Nancy and I are taking their son to Disneyland. I've never been and am hoping the presence of giant beloved characters from childhood strolling among us will help to restore some semblance of normalcy. Once in my room I sit and face the walls, unable to sleep. Today, you would pull out your phone and text "you can't believe what a nightmare this is" to every single person you know. But then you had to just sit with it. There was no way to get it out. Nobody to help you gauge your sanity.

We leave early the next morning for Disneyland. Nancy barely speaking. How was this the same person from the *Carla C*? I remembered Nancy as funny and kind and curious. Or was she just a person I talked to and our friendship was based only on the fact that she talked to me back? Who was this stranger driving me to the happiest place on earth?

Once there, Nancy finally opens up, she is planning on leaving Jack, she tells me. She cries and grabs my hand tightly as Cinderella asks us if we want a photo. I do, actually, but it's not the best time. I give Cinderella a look that implies "Can you maybe circle back around to us?" It is very difficult to enjoy Disneyland while someone tells you that their life has fallen apart. I try to be supportive, but really I'm barely twenty and freshly gay and a suburban thirty-five-year-old woman's unraveling marriage is not my idea of a sexy spring break. I should be in San Francisco on the lap of some flannel-wearing mustached slab of beef instead of trying to coax an unhappy schoolteacher onto Space Mountain. Besides, how well do I know this person? I would've been better off just knocking on any random door and staying with whoever would let me in. All these letters in the mail as worthless as supermarket flyers. Somehow we manage to get through the day. I cheerlead as best I can when I want nothing more than to get the fuck out of California. This state was clearly not for me.

The following day we again pick up the mother-in-law for a trip to the mall. Hell is other people. (That's Sartre. Another quote you should know.) Jack and the mother-in-law root through the housewares department of Nordstrom while Nancy and I look for baby things as I count down the hours until my flight home. I chatter inanely about how we don't have Nordstrom in New York and she tells me, "I'm leaving."

"What?"

"I'm leaving. Now. Tell them I've gone."

"You can't leave NOW."

"I can't take it any longer," she tells me. "I've got to go."

"But we're in Nordstrom. They're right over there," I say, pointing to Jack and the mother-in-law.

"I'm sorry." And she turns to leave.

"You can't go," I tell her firmly, panicked. "Not like this!" And she stops. She doesn't say anything. But she doesn't leave. And I find myself caught in the middle of something that unsettles me and I have no one to talk to. (And I guess she doesn't either, but I am too young to realize this. Or to help. Or do anything.)

Dinner repeats itself. Another horrible restaurant and more strained conversation. My patience for the mother-in-law now worn thin. I'm no longer quite so concerned with being the perfect guest. I meet her stare. You want to play this game, lady, let's play. Gay people are very good at cunty looks. We hone them like a musician practicing for the Philharmonic. (I give them now without even realizing. A slight shift in emotion and I'm suddenly Joan Crawford.) And before the meal ends that night, I hold the stare so long I get the mother-in-law to look away first. The waiter puts down our check.

"It's on me," I say, still holding the stare as she reaches for her coupons.

I am back in my room in their condo asleep when I feel something. A presence. And then an arm around my waist. Someone pressing against me and I jump. Nancy has crawled into bed with me, her hand on my thigh. I shoot out the other side of the bed. "What are you doing?!" She pats the mattress, as if I should join her. "I'm gay!" I blurt out. I've told very few people at this point, but I can see I need to wield it here. And then I make it seem as if I'm really torn up about coming out when in reality I'm not. It's like the best thing that's ever happened to me. But I need to shift the focus off of her and onto me. My only goal to get her out of this room. If there were a hotel I could walk to now, I would. I give up my secret so easily. Manufactured gay drama is my only way out of this situation. It seems to subdue her somewhat. My supposed unhappiness eclipsing hers for the moment. She tells me she wishes I could stay here with them in Long Beach forever before she finally retreats to her room. The sadness lingers long after she's gone.

The next morning is my flight back to New York. I walk into breakfast as if nothing has happened, when Nancy tells me my flight has been delayed. It feels like someone has punched me in the face. "My flight has been delayed?"

"Yes," she says, "they don't know when it's leaving. Why don't you stay another day?" If I had to crawl to the airport on my hands and knees at this point, I would. I say I would prefer to go now anyway. That I have to get home. And she finally relents, and Nancy and Jack and the baby drive me to the airport. And I say goodbye very quickly, I remember that. And I know I'm never going to see them again and I'm never going to write to Nancy again. "Thanks for everything," I say, grabbing my backpack as I disappear into the terminal.

A few weeks later, when I have stopped thinking about this, and the whole experience has been reduced to a tidy anecdote, I get a letter from Nancy. The envelope is quite thick. The thickest letter I have ever received. And I never open it.

# Commencement
# Address

FIRST OFF, I WANT TO SAY CONGRATULATIONS,
graduates! You did it! That's the good news. The
bad news is nothing you just did is going to prepare you
for anything that happens after today. If anyone told you
it *would* prepare you, well, they were lying. The last four
years have been one long charade. Everyone going along
with the ruse. Acting as if you were being readied for success in your career. And every choice you made in these

four years was instrumental in that success. I'm sorry to be the one to tell you that that is complete bullshit. Also bullshit, you *can't* really do anything you put your mind to and *one* person doesn't make a difference. Of course there are exceptions to every rule. But we're not here to talk about exceptions, we're here to talk about you. Basically you're in for a rude awakening. I know this is a bitter pill to swallow, especially on such a joyous occasion as this, but I wish whoever had spoken to me on my graduation day had at least prepared me, somewhat, for the terrible years that were to follow. Whatever your major was, that, as of today, is of no concern to anyone. Nobody will ever ask you or care. Sorry. (Maybe you'll get asked it in a job interview, but I guarantee the interviewer will glaze over during your response. The only people who will ever really care are other recent graduates you meet at a party in the coming months. This is only because you are still learning basic conversational skills and are falling back on the only thing you have to talk about.) Most of what's going to happen after today, I'm sad to report, is confusion, fear, and crippling anxiety. None of you are getting jobs in your chosen field anytime soon, so put that misconception to rest right now. They're still backed up on jobs for graduates from 2014. You're going to have to take a crappy job probably very soon. Unless you're rich. In which case this has all just been something to do for you and God bless, your lifetime of alcoholism and dissatisfaction awaits you. But for the other 99.9 percent of you, things are about to get shitty fast. I would say enjoy the next weeks. Parties, packing, etc. But I'm guessing soon after that you'll need a job. You're not getting one in political science or sociology or communications. None of those words actually even mean anything in the outside world. Again, sorry. Also, you know how you were competing with everyone else in your school for top grades, or teaching assistantships, or the lead in the show? That was tough, right? Well, now you're going to be competing with the entire world. And that's a whole lot tougher. I guess nobody told you this before because, well, it's a lot to take in. Who's the best actor in your graduating class? Raise your hand, please. Come on, don't be shy. Ah. There you are. Hi. You're probably never going to be a famous actor. Or even get a part. Like people graduating Julliard and Yale School of Drama can't get work, so think about it. Yeah. It's tough to hear, I know. Those shows you just did the past four years are things you'll reflect on in three decades when you're middle-aged and depressed. They will either make you feel better or worse, depending on your level of depression. Again, there are exceptions to every rule. But the odds are you're not one of them. I'm guessing most of you will be working in the service industry within a few weeks and will be wondering how that happened. Well, it happened because there aren't that many jobs and your major was likely stupid. I hope you had a lot of sex and drank a lot. That was the best thing you could have done to prepare yourself for your twenties, which is mostly drinking and sex. And if it's not, it should be. Because nothing else will be happening. Your early twenties, though, will be okay. You have a bit of leeway to "figure things out." The first few Thanksgivings you go home for, you can get away with saying things like "I want to get life experience first" and "I'm saving to backpack through Thailand." It's only when you get around twenty-seven that they will begin to get truly worried. That is when you will really dread going home for the holidays. It's not very festive to talk about your job waiting tables after having spent over two hundred thousand dollars on tuition. Debt so deep you'll never get out of it unless you win the lottery. Which you won't (and if you do, you would likely blow it all and then commit suicide, like most lottery winners). The real dread comes when you approach thirty and you feel like you've been going backward instead of forward. Now you'll realize you don't actually even know what it is you want to do. You'll start avoiding family members to avoid questions as you sink even further into debt. Perhaps you'll even consider going back to school to get another useless degree. If only to have something to talk about when people ask what you're up to that doesn't make them cringe. To compound the misery, also by this time you are unlikely to have found a significant other. Your years of slutting around leaving you ill-equipped with the tools you'll need to foster a nurturing relationship. The walls will feel like they're closing in on you. Your friends will all seem to be doing better, but trust me, they, too, will be drowning. Each tiny hard-won success—a job, a promotion, a wedding, a child—will prove to be its own little hell. In order to survive you will have to disconnect from the hopeful person you are today. All those conversations you had late into the night these past four years about what you will do in the future, well, none of that's going to happen. Let me see, how best to describe to you what it's going to be like after today. I know. Pretend you've never waited tables before. You have *no* experience whatsoever. And now, you are about to be waiting dozens of tables with the most demanding customers in the busiest restaurant in the world. Figuring out everything as you go. With no break. Ever. Until you die. That kind of sums up life after today. This safe little baby world you've been living in will be gone forever once you leave here. Everything from this day forward is going to be scrambling. Fumbling to keep up. Pay your bills. Figure out what you want to do. Who you want to be. I wish I could help you, I really do. But I can't. That's the messed-up thing. Nobody can. You only have you. But here are some other things that are true. Paying for your first apartment by yourself is amazing. Nothing is better than being independent. Making your own decisions. Don't blame others when things go wrong. That will be useful to know. Also, learn to apologize. And take criticism. When it's helpful. And when it's not, fuck it. Your instincts are always right. If you don't love what you're doing you won't be successful at it. Unless you're extremely good-looking. Don't peak too early. And don't be too hard on yourself. You still have roughly eight summers in your twenties ahead of you. There is nothing more beautiful than a summer in your twenties. Cherish each one. It's okay to not figure out what you want to do until you're thirty. Or even later. Whenever is actually okay. Don't ever not do anything because you're afraid of failing. Failing is fine. I used to be terrified of it. It's actually not a big deal, and sometimes a relief. Don't lie to yourself. Work hard. Don't be an asshole. Not everything has to happen immediately. Play the long game. Hang around people who value you. Don't be in a relationship just for the sake of it. It's okay to be alone. Go to the theater. Look at art. Read. These are the important things. Making time for coffee with a friend who feels like shit is also important. Always visit someone in the hospital. Always go to weddings and funerals. Everything else you can skip. Get a dog. Walk. Whenever you have the opportunity to go on a trip, take it. See the world. Always be willing to change your mind. Try. Try. Try.

# Sister Wilma

I GO TO ST. MEL'S GRAMMAR SCHOOL AND IT DOESN'T have a gymnasium. They ran out of money when they were building the school, so what was supposed to originally be the gymnasium became the church. Therefore, there were no phys ed classes. If that isn't proof there's a fucking God I don't know what is.

But then something terrible happened. I went to high

school. And St. Francis Prep did indeed have a gymnasium. School was hellish enough as it was, but the idea of having to interrupt the day and change out of your regular clothes into other clothes to have to throw a ball around for forty-five minutes was so unimaginable to me that you might as well have asked me to catch and skin a rabbit. And to make matters worse, since I had never actually taken a gym class before, I was completely inept at everything. The rules to any sport as indecipherable to me as ancient Greek. I could spit out the lyrics to *Sweeney Todd* at the drop of a hat but held a basketball with the same horror you would a severed head. Going into a locker room for the first time at the age of fourteen, I felt not unlike how I imagine Martha Stewart must have felt, years later, arriving in prison. Nothing in our previous lives could have possibly prepared us for this.

I approached my locker the way Brad Davis approached his jail cell in *Midnight Express*. This isn't happening. A horrible mistake has been made. I had not been caught smuggling drugs through Turkey like Brad Davis had, and yet here I was. My fate now to be determined by the capriciousness of a random phys ed teacher. A mediocre, disgruntled former athlete at best, a psychopath at worst. I changed into my gym clothes with the bashfulness of a geisha. A music hall burlesque performer from the 1890s showed more skin than I did. If anyone got so much as a glimpse of my bare shoulder I would've been surprised. Taking one shirt off and replacing it with another with the skill of a circus contortionist. I made such a concerted effort to look only at my locker and not at any of the other boys that if a gunman had entered the room I still wouldn't have turned my head.

Freshman year wasn't too bad. We were required to take track, badminton, and square dancing. All gay people can run, so no problem there. Badminton nobody could really play, so that wasn't a problem either. And square dancing, well, God knows why the fuck we were taking that. Was it an '80s thing? I had no clue. Neither did anyone else. But needless to say I was in heaven. "This is so dumb," I'd state to whoever happened to be standing next to me, while inside I was furiously memorizing each move. "Allemande left, do-si-do, and promenade!" After two classes I was ready to move to Texas. The short period of my life where I was taking square dancing was perhaps the most carefree time of my entire childhood. I had cast myself in *Dancing with the Stars* decades before the show even existed. And I was taking home the mirror ball. I was actually *good* at something in gym. Others would look at me to study my footwork. At fourteen I was already being prepared for line dancing in gay bars.

How thoughtful of the Franciscan brothers who ran the school. If they threw a circuit party it couldn't have been any gayer. Maybe this isn't going to be so bad after all, I allowed myself to think. Maybe I could do whatever they threw at me and just didn't know it yet.

But everything changed my sophomore year. What sick fuck would think to follow square dancing with football? In what universe did these two things even coexist much less fall under the same subject heading in a school curriculum. One is light, fun, joyous. The other instilling more fear than a home invasion. Just hearing a football game on television caused me anxiety. Everything seemed like it could break out into chaos at any moment. The heightened aggressiveness felt unsafe, even in my own living room. As if a foot could come through the TV and kick me in the face. I couldn't get far enough from the sound of it. Sitting in my room with the door closed and something normal on like *Hush, Hush, Sweet Charlotte* at full volume. Preferring to spend my Sunday afternoons with Bette Davis and Ingrid Bergman and Audrey Hepburn. Avoiding football games and any conversation associated with football took up more time than you'd think. And now I was expected to PLAY this game? Up until this point I had never thrown anything other than a fit.

The first day of football in gym class I decide to try to just blend in. Maybe they'll go over the rules for those who aren't familiar with them, I think to myself. I can't be the only one who doesn't know them. Maybe it's not as popular as I think it is. But, of course, it is more popular than I had even anticipated and there is no talk of rules, there is a complete understanding that this is a language we all speak. Except for me. The ball gets tossed around and everyone immediately appears to know what to do. Our phys ed teacher is not unkind, probably thirty, not unattractive, but let's just say he wasn't a distraction either. He barked at us in the way these men usually do. Acting out some masculine fantasy from their childhood no doubt. I was unimpressed. I wander off. I'm clearly not going to be able to blend in. I return to the locker room and change back into my clothes, then exit the school and walk the few blocks to Bloomingdale's, where I wander the aisles trying on outfits I can't afford. St. Francis Prep is in Fresh Meadows, Queens, right off the LIE and lucky for me it is a few short blocks from a multiplex, Bagel Nosh, and Bloomingdale's. When things get too much at school, or I need a break, I head out, grab a bagel, and poke through the sales rack of Perry Ellis shirts. One of the perks of blending into the background, having no friends, and doing everything alone is that I have basically become invisible. Nobody really notices if I skip a class or go to the bathroom after attendance and don't come back. If any of the salespeople think it's odd that a fifteen-year-old strolls in at 11:00 A.M. most school days to casually try on Calvin Klein jeans they never mention it. I nervously wonder as I hold a Lacoste shirt up to my chest for sizing how long I'll be able to avoid football. We have gym class twice a week and there are just so many times I can make a French exit before the phys ed teacher notices.

At home I start to consider my options going forward. The stress of how I'm going to continue getting out of gym class begins to eat away at me. Today, I could go online and learn the rules of football, watch a YouTube tutorial, and maybe have a chance of teaching myself, but then there was nothing. I couldn't ask anyone. It was too shameful. The night before my next gym class I decide I'm just going to go out there and do it. How hard could it be if these idiots can do it anyway? I mastered square dancing, I can master this. Fuck them.

After yet another sleepless night I show up for gym looking like a junkie. Tired and mentally exhausted I steel myself to do whatever is required as I run out onto the field in the freezing November air with my classmates. And the ball comes toward me and somebody screams, "Janetti!" (being addressed by my last name always sent a chill down my spine, nothing good comes of that) and I run away from it. This isn't going to work, I instantly realize. I can't just wish myself to play football. I head back to the locker room, humiliated. I hear whispers of "fag" as I retreat midclass. I will never go back.

I begin to plot my next course of action. Every second of every day I am consumed with one thought. Football. It sits on my chest like a piano. There's no way out, I think, except one. A physical injury that would preclude me from participating. That's when I decide I'm going to break my toe. A foot or an arm would be too extreme, and how would I even do it short of throwing myself from a moving car. No, a toe is just right. Small enough to not be of any great concern, but broken, would allow me to limp, get attention (a perk!), and with all certainty avoid gym class for several months. Besides, how difficult could it be to break a toe? I'll do it with one swift move. And the next thing I know I'm in our basement laundry room standing over my foot with a raised hammer like Kathy Bates in *Misery*. But when I bring the hammer down I move my foot at the last moment. I try several more times. The foot, with a mind of its own, continues to save itself at the last second. I've always had a low threshold for physical pain (all gay people do;

emotional pain, on the other hand, we are built for) and I've quickly discovered the fault in my plan. And then I think, *This is insane. I'm trying to hobble myself to avoid throwing a ball*. There's got to be another way. I have to be more clever. And then it comes to me.

The next time I have football in my schedule, instead of going to the gymnasium I head to the guidance counselor's office and tell her I need to speak with her immediately. Our guidance counselor is Sister Wilma, an ample woman of indeterminate age with a warm smile.

"Can I help you?" she asks.

"I need someone to talk to and I don't know where else to turn," I say, drama oozing out of every pore. She invites me in and we sit. Her office walls covered with travel photos, her coffee table stacked with celebrity magazines. I'm going to like it here. (Why the office was filled with copies of *People* and *Us* and not college brochures never crosses my mind.) She is at a chair placed in front of her desk and I am on the stained sofa. I begin. "My parents are getting divorced and I'm in a lot of pain." This, being a Catholic school, draws her in instantly.

"Go on," she prods.

First off, I should tell you right now, my parents aren't getting a divorce. They fought as most young Italian-American married couples did in the '70s and '80s. The word had been bandied about often enough in our house. But no, they were not getting a divorce. And if they were, nothing would have thrilled me more. To be a child of divorce—could there be anything more glamorous? Extra gifts, double holidays, a father who lived in an apartment on the other side of town who guiltily sought to buy my affection. What could be better? During the times my parents did fight and divorce was mentioned I found myself pushing my mother gently toward it. "Don't worry about me, do what's best for yourself." "I actually think this could be good for you." The selfless confidant. My sister was always more upset at the thought of it, while I was already mentally packing. A change of scenery would do us all good, I'd think to myself as I imagined my new sophisticated life as a child of divorce. Theater, cigarettes, late nights in convertibles. What any of this was based on I have no idea. But no, my parents aren't getting divorced and now here I am sitting in Sister Wilma's office, telling her how devastated I am at the destruction of our family. Sister Wilma makes us tea as I continue, never taking her eyes off me, afraid to miss one second of my increasingly lurid story.

"It's really bad," I pronounce vaguely.

"How bad?"

"I can't say. But bad." When she seems too overly

concerned I have to pull myself back a bit. "Bad. But not *bad* bad. Yet." I don't want to end up having child services or, worse, some well-meaning priest show up at our door. Nuns can be unpredictable. I have to play this one just right.

Fortunately, she couldn't be more delightful. At the end of our session, like any good soap opera, I leave on a cliff-hanger. "I'm also afraid of—oh, that's the bell."

She's practically salivating. "Afraid of what?!" I must be a nice change of pace from her usual stream of zit-covered, midlevel students stopping by for SAT worksheets and state university applications.

She says, "I'd like to see you again."

This is when I stop and turn, applying years of *One Life to Live* watching. "Oh, Sister, I don't know, I'm so afraid of falling behind in my studies. Especially with everything else that's going on." I tilt my head slightly down, then raise it for a moment, making a small concession. "I suppose I *could* come during gym classes . . ." And right then and there she fills out an excuse slip for next week's phys ed classes and beyond.

"I want you to come see me whenever you have gym," she says, handing me the slip. My life now saved by this small piece of paper. My most prized possession. "Don't lose it," she says. Lose it? I'll fucking sleep with it.

Now I suppose in hindsight I could have actually just told her the truth. I was certainly troubled enough without having to create this bit of theater. But the thought never even occurred to me. Also, I don't think reality had quite the same salaciousness as the tale I was already starting to spin.

I'm suddenly back in her office. This time she has our tea already prepared, and before long she's treating me more like a fellow nun who's stopped by to gossip than a fifteen-year-old closeted sophomore.

"Tell me everything," she says, settling in. "How's your mother doing?"

"Not great," I say, blowing on my tea. "I think we're going apartment hunting this weekend." I have my parents so far down the road to divorce I haven't quite figured how I'm going to get out of it when they never actually do.

"So, it's really happening," she says.

"Oh, God, yeah," then quickly adding, "I don't know what I'll do," remembering that I'm upset. I give my parents a complicated backstory that even I can't keep straight. Creating characters for them as rich as any I'd seen on prime-time TV. Arguments, long-held grudges, petty grievances, fits of hysteria.

"I thought you said your mother never drank," Sister Wilma says, catching me in one of my inconsistencies.

"This night she did," I say with great import. Eventually, I just start rehashing plotlines from *Knots Landing*.

My mother worked in a law office in the city. My father often traveled for his job as a sales manager for Cunard Line. Neither of them had any idea that I had cast them as the stars of my own private soap opera. I'd come home from school and catch the end of *One Life to Live* while fixing my lunch. When Viki moves out on Clint after suspecting him of cheating on her with a past lover I think, *That's good, I can use that*, as I spread mustard on my turkey sandwich.

If anything, my parents should be grateful. I had turned them into characters worthy of their own show. The John and Felicia that costarred in the story of my life as told to Sister Wilma were a wild, unpredictable, volatile pair. Think *Who's Afraid of Virginia Woolf?* meets *Hart to Hart*. If I ever felt even the slightest bit of guilt I have no memory of it.

As the weeks pass I'm able to steer the conversation away from my parents' disintegrating marriage and toward more banal topics like the weather or what I watched on TV the previous night. Having to keep this storyline moving was providing its own kind of stress. Some days I'd walk in and just not have it in me. "Can we just sit here," I'd say on those days. Sister Wilma now looking deflated. This was her own private telenovela after all and I was preempting this week's episode. But we had formed a fellowship by this time, and the falling away of my family drama didn't preclude us from happily chatting about whatever was on our minds. I looked forward to this time with Sister Wilma. Some days we'd just leaf through her old vacation albums and she would tell me about her summers in Nova Scotia. She started out an easy mark but ended up a friend.

On the last day of our sessions together Sister Wilma asks about my parents. We hadn't talked about them in a while at this point.

"Oh, they're fine," I say.

"You mean they're not getting divorced?"

"Nope."

"Huh."

"I know," I say casually, not feeling the need to explain myself further. She tells me I'm welcome back at any time, that her door is always open. But this day is also my last day of football in gym class. I no longer need to come. I no longer need her. She gives me my final excuse slip and hugs me goodbye (you could hug children then) and tells me she'll miss me.

And when I go to present this final slip to my phys ed teacher. The final slip that excuses me from the entire semester's worth of class. He takes it. And signs, or whatever it is he had to do with it, I don't remember. And then he holds this slip of paper back out to me. Hanging on to it for a moment where it remains floating between the two of us. And the way he looks at me while he does this tells me he knows that this has all been bullshit. He knows what I've done. What I am. And I feel somehow diminished. Less than. Dirty, even. My amusing little ruse now revealed to me as a pathetic trick played on a lonely nun. And I think . . . "What if I had stayed?" "What if I had learned?" "What if I had thrown the football?" And then I think, "fuck you," as I snatch the slip of paper from the air. I'd do it all again.

# Christmas

FOR ME, NO NIGHT OF THE YEAR WAS FILLED WITH more anticipation than Christmas Eve and no morning of the year was filled with more crushing disappointment than Christmas Day. Christmas Eve embodied the promise of all that could be. The possibility of gifts I hadn't even thought of, things I didn't even know that I wanted yet. And soon they would be mine. "OH MY GOD, I LOVE IT!" What these magical items were

I had no idea. But I was certain they were out there. Somewhere. What I was missing could surely be bought in a store for the right amount of money. Inevitably, the hope of Christmas Eve is followed by the reality of Christmas morning. My sister and I up at 6:30 A.M., my parents still asleep. We opened our gifts without them. I remember later seeing TV shows and movies where entire families would gather together around the tree and "ooh" and "ah" collectively as the children opened their presents in delight in front of their adoring parents. I couldn't think of anything worse. I didn't want any witnesses to the certain indifference I'd show as I tore through the wrapping paper only to reveal a game I'd never heard of.

"What is this?" I'd ask my sister, holding it out in front of me like a bag of dog shit. It was as if my parents were buying gifts for some other child. One who would appreciate a Hasbro toy that wasn't even popular enough to have its own commercial.

(Having to give a performance while opening a gift in front of the giver has never been one of my strong suits. The forced smile as I hold up a shirt that I hate. "Thank you, it's perfect." The giver always immediately sensing my dislike for whatever item it is that I've already reboxed and shoved aside. Offers from the giver to exchange it pour forth like a tap and the rest of our time together is now damage control.

"No, really, I love it, I don't have anything like it."

"Are you sure? Because it's not any trouble to return it."

"Of course I'm sure, I would tell you."

After a few more back-and-forths the visit never regains its proper footing. I much prefer to be in the position of gift *giver*. "Here. Don't open it in front of me, the receipt's taped to the bottom of the box." I don't need a show, thank you. A party where the birthday person opens up their presents in front of all the guests is perhaps the most grotesque thing that one adult person can do to another. I didn't even do this when I was six. The few birthday parties I had when I was very young I chose to open my gifts alone after everyone had gone home. There's only so much enthusiasm one can muster for a box of Colorforms.)

I guess there's something to be said for a family gathering around the tree to see the wonder on a young child's face as they yank the bow off a new bike. But I think it was better for all parties concerned that my parents never saw the look on my face as I lifted the lid off a box containing the wrong brand of sneakers or a watch I would never wear. Thankfully, I didn't have to put on a performance for my sister, my only audience member. She didn't care how ungrateful I was as she excitedly laced up her new ice skates.

"You want mine, too?" I'd ask dead-eyed, offering her my blue version of her pink ones. We lived in Queens not Canada, I wasn't planning on traveling by ice anytime soon.

And to make matters worse, as I got older I already knew exactly what gifts I was getting. Having spent the previous weeks going through every inch of the house in order to find them. One year there was a folded-up Ping-Pong table covered with a sheet barely concealed behind the hot water heater. I mean, come on! (Although to this day I'm still an excellent Ping-Pong player, so that one gets a pass.) Car trunk, parents' closet, dresser drawers, I knew all the spots. Occasionally, I'd find something two days before Christmas in a spot that had previously been empty. *Cutting it close*, I'd think. I tried not to look, to just wait until Christmas morning like a normal child, but I couldn't help myself. I was even a little annoyed once I found them. Like if you're going to hide something in your bedroom closet, you deserve having it discovered. *You're not even trying*, I'd think as I rifled through my mother's underwear drawer, revealing a backgammon set tucked under her bras. At least make it a little challenging. Short of burying our presents in the backyard I'm not sure where I really expected my parents to hide them. Our house wasn't that large so there were just so many options. But still . . .

There would always be a few items I missed, though. So there was still a surprise to be had on Christmas morning. And with that surprise came hope. What if this year were different? What if everything were different? Even now I don't know what it was that I actually wanted. To this day I'm hard-pressed to say what it is that I want when someone asks me. "I'll know it when I see it," I want to say. (One exception was my sixteenth birthday. I asked my parents for a leather jacket that year. And on my birthday, when I opened the box, inside there was a light gray leather blazer. I can still see it. I'm sure I made a face not unlike the one you make while taking a sip of orange juice when you think you poured milk. I told my mother that's not the kind of leather jacket I wanted. I was thinking *Rebel Without a Cause* not retired car salesman. She said this was the last gift she was ever getting me. And it was. True to her word I haven't received one since. Gift cards for the past thirty-five years, yes. But she was no longer going to make the effort to go out and buy something for me. She'd had enough of my shit. And, really, who could blame her? Even at the time I remember thinking, *Good for you.* I know I wouldn't have shopped for me.)

But the night before Christmas was perfect. Anything was possible. If I could bottle one hour it would be the hour before I went to bed on Christmas Eve. Usually I wasn't able to sleep because of the excitement and I would bring my blanket and my teddy bear and make a nest on the floor of my sister's bedroom. Whispering to each other throughout the night as it dragged on for an eternity. There were so many things I couldn't imagine. And one of them could be right outside that door, in our very own living room, just waiting for me to open it. And change my life forever.

# Tan

I DON'T KNOW HOW IT STARTED. BUT AT SOME POINT all I ever wanted to be was tan. I worked toward that goal with the same kind of round-the-clock dedication as a medical intern. When someone would compliment my tan I would thank them with a sense of pride more befitting a violin prodigy or Oscar winner. Not someone whose only accomplishment was lying in the sun nine hours a day.

I grew up in the '70s before we had suntan lotion. It might have been found in some households, but it was mostly seen as a luxury item more commonly used by idiots who had nothing better to do with their money. Who in their right mind would want to cover up the sun? I think the highest SPF at the time was 2. Any sun product we did have was basically a form of oil or butter. More suited to cooking the skin than protecting it. The thought of blocking the sun's rays as nonsensical as swimming in a down coat. Parents didn't put sunscreen on babies or children either. They didn't even watch them when they went into the water. You pretty much had a fifty-fifty chance of returning safely from a trip to the beach. We sat out exposed to the elements all day like shipwreck survivors or lizards. If the sun didn't kill you, the ocean would. Some days I'd get knocked down and dragged by the waves so many times I'd stagger out of the water looking like I'd just been mugged. My mother barely glancing up from her Peter Benchley novel. She oddly stayed in the shade. Protected her skin like Greta Garbo (think Nicole Kidman), which was quite unusual for an Italian-American woman in the '70s, who were more likely to be a shade of crisp bacon for the months of July and August. But not my mother. Always under an umbrella with a book and a hat while my sister and I sat in the sand as the sun blisters rose up on our shoulders and arms like Bubble Wrap. Popping each tiny bump as little droplets of water dripped out. The new skin raw underneath. Then burning that layer, too. My T-shirts coated with enough dead skin at the end of each day to make a wallet. There were years where I still had a tan at Christmas.

But it wasn't until I reached college age that I truly started perfecting tanning. The beginnings of what would later become an art form. A tan was no longer just something that happened to me by the end of the summer; it became my job. A job that I took very seriously. Had I pursued my studies with the same kind of vigor I brought to tanning I could have graduated magna cum laude from Harvard instead of with a B.A. from Hofstra.

For some reason, while I was in college in the '80s on Long Island, students wore shorts year-round. No matter that our winters rivaled Winnipeg. I don't know if this is something that college students still do. I no longer go to colleges because they make me feel old. There's nothing that can disabuse you faster of the notion that you're still young than walking onto a college campus once you're past forty.

"Oh, my God, they're all children," I said to myself the last time I visited one. I had no idea. I thought I was

the same when I was in college as I am now. An adult.
But I was about as similar to an adult when I was strut-
ting around the campus grounds as one of the squirrels.
A barely formed little half-wit who was under the delu-
sion that he was a grown person. Do professors spend
the whole day laughing at their students? I would. Walking around, so cocky, like they know it all, when in fact
college students are nothing more than high school students with three less pimples.

Any day that would hit above sixty degrees I would
strip off my shirt and lie out on the quad grass as if I were
in St. Tropez. One year it was particularly warm during
spring break and I laid out each day like I was clocking
in to shift work at an automotive factory. "Oh, shit, I've
got to go," I'd say the second the sun was over the grass,
as if someone were waiting to dock my pay if I missed
even one minute of prime tanning time. By the end of
that spring break I was so tan everyone thought I'd been
to Cancun. The awe on their faces when I replied, "No,
I just stayed on campus."

"You got that tan on campus?!"

"Yep." The achievement in my mind only that much
more impressive, considering I hadn't left Hempstead,
Long Island.

As college came to a close and most of my fellow

graduates began to plan for their careers and futures my immediate objective was to determine how to stay tan year-round. Hopscotching from summers at the beach to winter breaks in the Caribbean and Mexico, spaced out enough so that as one tan faded another was ready to take its place.

My first order of business after graduation was taking the typical backpack-through-Europe trip. No Scandinavian countries for me, thank you. I didn't have one precious day to waste in soggy Copenhagen. The thought of needing an umbrella was enough to make me sick. No, this was to be a trip of Mediterranean delights. One where the chance of sunshine each day hovered at around 98 percent. If it was a country where I couldn't get by with only shorts and a tank top, I wasn't interested. I take all the money I get from my graduation party. (The only reason I had one. Collecting envelopes from my relatives as though I'm manning the register of an express lane. "Next!") I'm going to start off in Spain and then five weeks later meet up with my friend Sal in Greece. Sal is also Italian-American and gay, and we had previously been involved for about five minutes. But with all the drama that young, gay Italians on Long Island could infuse them with. Acting out our shitty little soap opera for each other until we got bored.

And now here I am, twenty-two, with my backpack, boarding a plane to Madrid (a charter airline so low budget the flight attendants wore their own clothes), where I am to meet my friend Laura, who is just finishing up a semester abroad in Edinburgh (another wet city I pass on). I send a letter to Laura weeks ago with my flight information and she sends me a letter back saying she'll meet me at baggage claim. This was the equivalent of texting then. It was slow but efficient.

On a hot summer afternoon I arrive in Madrid, where we are to spend a few days seeing the sights. But after one morning of museum-going I'm already getting itchy. The sun is blazing outside and I'm at the Prado looking at Goyas like a dope. Since Laura and I have no firm plans over the next weeks I suggest we take off the next day for Seville. A city more suited to lazing by swimming pools than Madrid. Ideally, I'm looking for someplace where I can see the sights from a lounge chair. I don't let her know quite how manic I am about my tanning hours. I realize I will sound insane enough in short order, so I do my best to pretend that I'm normal. That I, too, am traveling to see every European artwork and cathedral I have ever studied and not to lay out until my skin is the texture of a Louis Vuitton handbag.

We spend a week traveling through southern Spain.

Staying in youth hostels or rooms that we rent. But I want to go even farther south than Spain. Someplace where the heat is strong enough to knock you unconscious. I have always wanted to go to Morocco ever since seeing *The Man Who Knew Too Much* when I was a child. Jimmy Stewart and Doris Day travel to Marrakech, where their kid gets abducted and Doris Day has to sing "Que Sera, Sera" to get it back. I always remembered how exotic and fabulous it looked. The kind of backdrop that could provide both international intrigue and sun strong enough to get the job done. We find a youth hostel in our travel bible, *Let's Go Europe* (I know Morocco's not in Europe, but it was in the book, so calm down. I will return at a future point in this essay to the topic of *Let's Go Europe*. I cannot overstate its importance), that we are told is frequented by Peace Corps volunteers and that also has a rooftop sunning deck. I can't think of anything more ideal. I'll probably meet some gorgeous, selfless, farm-fed midwestern volunteer who's on a weekend holiday. Swapping stories half-naked on plastic loungers as we leisurely sun ourselves in one hundred and ten–degree heat.

Laura and I take the ferry from Algeciras to Tangier. I should mention that Laura is fair-skinned and at this point in our travels still appears to be blissfully unaware of the true purpose of this trip. I tan myself on the ferry as we play cards. One deck of cards is like traveling with Netflix. Hours of entertainment right at our fingertips. And we met people while traveling, too. Collected them like matchbooks. Each new person an exciting adventure. I would talk to anyone. Of course now this sounds like the most awful thing in the world. I'm constantly maneuvering myself through life to be the farthest away as possible from people. If I can hear your voice you're too close. But then, having been an adult for all of one minute, other people were still a novelty. "You live where? What's *that* like? Do you want to share our room tonight?" Somebody I met ten minutes ago could inspire a fiercer loyalty than any I feel today for people I've known for over thirty years. "We have to wait for Jean-Louis and Colette!" I'd find myself insisting on numerous occasions while traveling when in my twenties. The names would change but the devotion would not.

On this particular ferry ride, Laura and I meet a woman from Sweden. The fact that she happens to be on line in front of us for café con leche is apparently enough to bond us for life. We tell Sigrid about our youth hostel and suddenly the three of us are inseparable.

"Where's Sigrid? We're not leaving without her!" I can remember nothing of Sigrid aside from her name,

I'm assuming she had a personality. All I can recall, though, is including her in everything. We must've liked something about her. Although that wasn't exactly a prerequisite when meeting people while traveling when you're twenty-two. I'm sure now I probably would have found her insufferable after two seconds. But what did I know then? I'd spend hours talking to strangers. Asking them questions. Learning about their lives. Today I can think of nothing that would fill me with more dread. Maybe I met enough people over the years to realize that they just start repeating themselves after a while. So you're never really meeting someone new. Just another version of someone else you know. "I already have one of you," I often find myself thinking while talking to a person I've just met.

But twenty-two-year-old Gary is a Chatty Cathy. He adores new people. Can't get enough of them. Will start a conversation with a doorknob. (Occasionally, twenty-something Gary still comes out when traveling—"Oh, hey, what's your name, where are you from?"—and then fifty-something Gary swats him back down. "Are you out of your mind!?")

Laura, Sigrid, and I arrive in Tangier and transfer to a bus that will take us on to Marrakech. What I imagine the youth hostel to look like and what it actually looks like are two very separate things that share no common ground. My Club Med fantasy replaced with a concrete structure that appears plucked directly from East Germany. We stay in slablike rooms and share a hallway bathroom. But there is a roof deck (decades before they were made famous by millennials) that looks out over the medina. And it is gorgeous. Suddenly, I'm in *The Man Who Knew Too Much*. Snake charmers and dentists, musicians and food stalls all jammed together in one great big outdoor plaza. And us looking out over it all. There are plastic chairs and tepid beers and the sun is setting and there are Peace Corps volunteers. Just like I had read about in *Let's Go Europe*. (A book that held more adventures than any one life could contain. A new edition came out every year. Thousands and thousands of places to see, stay, eat. I don't know why, but it was infinitely more exciting arriving at a hotel you read about in *Let's Go Europe* than at one you find online.) And we all mingle. Like the most perfect college party you could imagine in the most extraordinary location. The heat a balmy ninety degrees as the sun dips behind the Atlas Mountains. My fantasy not so far off after all.

The next morning, we go to a local market and get fresh juice and about ten minutes after that I'm in the shared bathroom of our hostel with the worst diarrhea of my life. I spend the next several days in a fever dream going from bed to toilet (I use the term loosely) to bed again. "Que Sera, Sera" indeed. Laura and Sigrid come and go, checking in on me periodically. And in the rare moments when I am completely lucid all I can think is, *I'm losing my tan*. This fear propels me back to health. I refuse to sweat several weeks of sun off me on a mattress no thicker than a Kleenex. Once I have enough strength I'm lying flat on my back on the roof, letting the sun roast me like one of the rotating chickens in the medina. Laura wonders if this is wise. I tell her to mind her own business, I'm fine. So what if I lost ten pounds in two days.

After a week of mostly shitting, it's time to leave Morocco. And one last time we are on the roof. And I talk to a boy. And he's in the Peace Corps. And he looks like I want him to look. And I ask questions and we laugh and we drink and it's hot. And he introduces me to his friends, and I, to mine ("You'll LOVE Sigrid!") and the night goes on and nothing happens. And I still wonder why.

We part with Sigrid once we get back to Spain. We exchange addresses. Promise to visit. Miss her terribly when she's gone. And then a few days later it's like she never existed.

Laura and I make our way through Spain and the south of France and Italy. Picking up various Gustavs and Fleurs and Lorenzos along the way. I forgo trips to castles and museums in order to sun. Still secretly trying to make up for my lost days in Morocco. Until it's time for Laura to now depart and for me to head to Greece to meet Sal. Laura, still pale, still unaware of the real reason for this trip after over a month. Bless her.

I have a week on my own before Sal arrives and I ferry to Corfu, where I meet two young women traveling together, best friends Jen and Diane. And we rent a very cheap apartment from a woman holding up a sign as we arrive on the dock. And it's a few blocks from the beach. And there's a kitchen and we cook dinners. Wouldn't it be nice to be that uncomplicated again? To cook dinner with someone I don't know. To share a home. To be close. If for only a short while. It's like a dream I'm surprised I still remember. Maybe the truth is they annoyed me. And it was a cheap way to travel. And they were company for a few days. A way to get me from one part of my trip to the next. This is all possible. But that's not how I remember it. I remember laughing with Jen and Diane and talking late into the night and packing lunches to bring to the beach together. And going to an outdoor movie starring Montgomery Clift and Elizabeth Taylor. And buying bags of figs that we leave in a bowl on the kitchen table. And I tell Jen and Diane that I'm gay. This somehow is still cause for an entire evening's worth of conversation at twenty-two. And for this week we are a small family. And I am grateful that there was no email or Facebook or Instagram to keep us in touch with each other. Trying to hold on to something that has already dissolved like cotton candy the second it's over. Some things are meant to last a week when you're twenty-two. They are not meant to be held on to. They rot and curdle when kept past their expiration dates. I don't remember their faces now. Only the feeling.

I meet Sal at the airport in Athens. (Again, letters exchanged, a text that takes four weeks to come through.) He walks right by me with his backpack. "You're so tan! I didn't even recognize you!" Good, I think, I'm halfway there. We spend five weeks traveling through the Greek Islands. In my mind I am trying to re-create the movie *Summer Lovers*, where Peter Gallagher and Daryl Hannah have a threesome with a random French woman. It's not the threesome I'm trying to re-create so much as the freedom. There is nothing more wonderful than spending a summer going from island to island in the Mediterranean when you're young. Nothing comes close. We rent little rooms in each place—Paros, Crete, Santorini—and Sal makes us breakfasts and we ride mopeds, spend hours in the sea.

I don't meet a boy on this trip, though. This bridge between college and the rest. I don't fall in love. I don't anything. We spend our final night in Mykonos. Another dinner with people we have just met. Still feeling the warmth of the sun on my face at midnight.

# Destination Wedding

I F THERE'S ANYTHING WORSE THAN RECEIVING AN invitation to a destination wedding I haven't experienced it. I don't know where and how these started. When I was a child my parents went to weddings and came back the same night, not three days later. They didn't have to book a fucking airline ticket. Usually returning with candy-coated almonds in white netting and a matchbook with the names of the bride and groom on it, not luggage.

In the '70s children didn't go to weddings, they were grown-up events. People could smoke and drink in peace. They hardly interacted with their children at home much less in public. At the time, my parents attending a wedding was akin to them hosting the Met Gala. Nothing in our lives could match the glamour of the day of a wedding. My mother in her mink stole, my father his tux. Spritzed in cologne and perfume they clicked out of our house and drove to Long Island or Brooklyn or New Jersey. And they sat at tables with assigned seats and were served steak or fish and danced to a live band. Later the bride and groom would visit each table. The bride holding a pillowcase for the guests to drop their envelopes into. (These were usually Italian-American weddings, money was the preferred gift, and the couple went around collecting checks like Halloween candy.) I had no firsthand experience of weddings. They existed only in my imagination.

My mother always decreed the next day that the wedding was lovely. I was desperate for details, but to get any more information out of my mother you'd have to waterboard her. She did not gossip or often say unkind things about others, which was unfortunate for me, as that was all I wanted to hear. To her these were adult affairs, not to be discussed with children. Which only made them that much more enticing, my mind concocting opulent soirees out of *The Great Gatsby* (which I knew from the paperback cover and the Robert Redford/Mia Farrow film I saw at seven).

It wasn't until I went to my first wedding as a teenager at Leonard's of Great Neck on Long Island (a reception hall that was more like Teresa Giudice's home on *The Real Housewives of New Jersey* than Gatsby's mansion, which, to add insult to injury, is also located on Long Island) that I realized just how much my imagination overshot reality. I don't know quite what I was expecting. But certainly nothing that had competing brides in different rooms of the same reception hall. "You mean there's more than *one* wedding going on here at the same time?" My jaw dropped to the mint-green carpeted ground. *What could be less special than that,* I thought at fifteen. (This was one of the first in many lessons I would receive that real-life experiences rarely match what we imagine them to be in our heads. The following years are to be a constant stream of disappointments and mental readjustments. The only thing that's exactly how you picture it in your head is Venice. It *is* that magical. Everything else falls short.)

Like most people, the first round of weddings I attend

as an adult is in my mid-twenties. This is when many of your friends from high school and college embark on their starter marriages. (Anyone who gets married in their twenties will not be in their forties. This is a fact.) Going to weddings in your twenties is not without its perks. Free dinner. Dancing. And in most cases an open bar. If you find yourself at a wedding with a cash bar you can be certain that this will be the only topic of conversation among the guests. Indignant whispers spreading across the rented hall like wildfire. Being unable to afford an open bar should be your first indicator that this marriage is headed for disaster. If the fondest memory you're creating involves guests rummaging through their pockets trying to cobble enough bills together to pay for a gin and tonic you're setting a very low bar for the rest of your life.

(A strange thing about the weddings you attend when you're young that you don't realize at the time because, well, you're young and you have, like, not much to go by, is that this is likely the last time you will see the bride and groom. In many ways a wedding is like a goodbye to your friend and the person they're marrying that you inevitably dislike. (Occasionally, you will like both members of the couple. These are the marriages that will fizzle out the quickest.) The friend you were barely interested in now has a partner that you care even less about. Sometimes you hold on to the friendship a bit past the wedding. Go through several long and torturous rescheduled dinners where you discover you have less and less in common. Maybe make it to the first pregnancy. But I find it best to cut the cord right then and there at the reception. Give your gift and wish them well. If it's meant to be your friend will resurface after the divorce.)

Weddings were often a harmless diversion. An activity that allowed you to talk shit about people you hardly see, wonder why you were invited, and complain about the food. But something hideous happened over the decades, and what was once a local evening of dress-up and boozing transformed itself into a faraway, multiday activity-laden obligation that more closely resembled a corporate retreat. I didn't even want to go to a wedding when it involved a drive longer than an hour, already planning my escape before I've even left the house. But now, air travel is involved. This is also something you are expected to pay for and take time off work for. It's like asking a stranger on the street to plan your vacation and then handing them your credit card. (I feel similarly about destination weddings as I do cash bars. Unless you are paying to have us all travel on private jets and stay in our own villas, knock it off.) The wedding will still be the same god-awful affair. Trite speeches that everyone thinks are clever, cringe-worthy toasts and mind-numbing conversations with someone else's relatives. I don't want to have dinner with you the night before your wedding. And I certainly don't want to have brunch with you the day after it. There are only so many times one can dodge the same people. Hiding behind walls in hotel hallways until the mother of the groom and her sister pass. A person you innocently talk to the night before now becomes a booby trap you have to avoid for the rest of the trip. Any social event is rife with enough awkward moments. To stretch one out from a Thursday through Monday is unconscionable. I don't believe I know any human being well enough that they should feel comfortable asking me to fly to the Bahamas for a piece of chicken.

There's also something about people professing their love for each other in public that makes me inherently uncomfortable. It's just so . . . personal. We wouldn't be expected to watch them have sex, why do we have to hear them talk about all the intimate details of their relationship? Other than their therapist I can't imagine who this would be of interest to. All brides and grooms are total narcissists, the universe revolving around them. Their love story so unique (even though it sounds like every other one), they are the stars and we are their supporting cast whose part it is to fawn and laugh on cue. To compliment and cry. To be joyful. To make this perfect for them. And that is a lot of pressure to put on people who had to change planes and drive in a minivan with strangers in order to reach an event space that ends up looking remarkably similar to any number of ones back home.

But perhaps I only feel this way because I never thought I could get married as a child. Marriage was something that was never going to be a part of my life. Was never for me. This was reserved for other people. Whose love mattered more than mine ever would. Mine counted for less. Had no value. Was funny, even. Made people uncomfortable. Which is maybe why their love made me uncomfortable. And maybe I was jealous. Of what I couldn't have. Of counting for less when they seemed to count for so much more.

Then the world spins. And spins and spins and spins some more and slowly, so slowly there is change. And now I have someone in my life, have had someone for many years. And my love suddenly is something that I, too, can celebrate. And I understand something that I perhaps didn't before. Not really. There is power in saying to your friends and family. To the world. "I love this person. I want to share this with you. I want you to know me."

And this someone in my life, this man, Brad, becomes my husband when I am fifty. And in front of our families we profess our love for each other. This intimate thing now seems okay to share. More than okay, wonderful. (Shame is a hard thing to shake off when it has been baked in for so long.) And this wedding, our wedding, takes place on a fourteen-day cruise in the middle of the Caribbean. I mean if you're going to do a destination wedding, fucking do it.

# Grandma

I TAKE MY MOTHER AND HER SISTER TO LUNCH IN THE
city recently. I want to hear more about their mother,
my grandmother, who died two weeks before I was born.
I had gathered bits and pieces over the years but never
all at once. When I was a child, my sister and I couldn't
ask my mother about our grandmother. She was unable
to talk about her. Years later she would sometimes say,
"My mother used to make it like this," usually referring

to pie crust or meatballs or sauce or, "I learned how to sew from my mother." Little clues that I would gather and hold close. If I were ever to press a bit further she would become emotional and change the subject. So I never did.

I thought about my grandmother though, Lena was her name, often when I was young. The dead can be so much more interesting than the living. This woman who had died so close to my birth. Would she have liked me? I was certain I would have liked her. In my mind she was perfect. My mother had lost her father the year before her mother, so by the time I was born she was an orphan. It's not exactly Dickens but it was still sad. And yet it made my mother that much more fascinating to me. There was nothing to compare her against. Nobody to tell us stories of when she was young. No opportunity to see her defer to someone else. What would that have been like? To see her with her mother? Strange, now it would seem to me. I liked having her all to myself. (Big surprise, the gay child wants all their mother's attention. My earliest memory is my father taking my sister to see *The Sound of Music* when I'm two years old and after they go turning to my mother like, "I thought they'd never leave.")

My grandmother came from Italy when she was a

little girl. At lunch, my mother and my aunt Santa tell me the story of how she came to America.

"Her mother, our grandmother," Aunt Santa tells me, "was waiting for her husband to send money to Italy for them to come over. But she found out from someone in their village that her husband, our grandfather, was living with another woman in America. So she sold their farm and with the money she got they crossed over on an ocean liner to New York."

She was pissed. You do not fuck with the women in my family. Apparently, she showed up with their two children to where he was living with his mistress and kicked the mistress out. This was my seven-year-old grandmother's introduction to America. My mother, while picking at her salmon, remembers that their mother had talked to them about the crossing to America. "Oh, she had a great time on that trip." How desperate they must've been to take such a gamble. To leave everything forever. What was my great-grandmother thinking on those long days across the ocean? As she sailed toward nothing certain except an unfaithful husband.

But this is how my grandmother comes to this country. Holding the hand of a woman who came here to fight for what was hers. For what had been promised to her children. A future. And this woman who grabbed her two children by the hand, who leaves behind everything she knows, everything she had, is also grabbing me by the hand and dragging me to today. To New York, to Los Angeles, to this computer.

My grandmother Lena gets married when she is young. And my mother tells me that when she and her sister are children they find in a box a marriage certificate between their mother and someone who is not their father.

"She had been married before," my mother tells me. Now I had heard this story already, that my grandmother had been divorced but never really talked much about it. Italian-Americans do not get divorced. Certainly not in the 1930s. It was incredibly taboo, almost unheard of. My grandmother left her husband because he physically abused her. I knew that had been the reason, but the enormity of what that must have meant at the time had never really sunk in. Leaving her husband was a scandal. *She* was scandalous. And yet she never looked back. How extraordinary. Everything around her was built to tell her she must stay. And she didn't. And eventually she met my grandfather, who was recently widowed and had two children of his own, who were being raised by his deceased wife's parents as he worked as an icebox man and saved money. But once he married my grandmother, his in-laws wouldn't let him have his children back. His own children. They did not want them raised by a divorced woman. She was considered less than by them. Unfit. There was a custody hearing and my grandfather lost.

"One day Mom took us to their house, do you remember, Felicia?" Aunt Santa asks her. My mother says yes but looks less sure of the details than my aunt. My mother is the younger of the sisters. "But you were too afraid to come to the door with us," Aunt Santa continues, "so I went with Mom. And one of the sons answered, I don't know which one. And he wouldn't let us in. But Mom tried to convince him to see his father and he took our number and promised he would call but never did. I'm sure they're both dead by now." And this is how my mother sees her half-brother for the only time in her life. Glimpsed through a cracked door from the sidewalk.

Nothing so exciting ever happened in our immediate family. I would've killed to find out one of my parents had a secret child. Unfortunately for me all the best drama had been poured into the previous generation.

"Everyone loved our mother," my aunt continues. "The whole neighborhood." Sometimes, in the way somebody tells you something, you know it's true.

They grew up in a railroad apartment on East Eighty-Second Street without any heat. This is something I did not previously know. "Oh, you were poor," I say. They both look at each other considering, then: "We weren't poor," my aunt says.

"You didn't have heat."

"Yes, but we always had food."

My mother and her sister went to Catholic school, and the convent where the nuns lived was across the street from their building. "When the nuns wanted us to do something they would clap through the windows for us and we had to come down and do whatever they asked," my aunt tells me. They were close with the other children on the block. Two of them eventually married and became my godparents, Pat and Vinny (my middle name is Vincent). One of the nuns took a dislike to my mother. Sister Letitia. My mother makes a sour face when talking of her almost seventy years later:

"Whenever we saw her or one of the other nuns we had to bow and say, 'Praise be Jesus Christ, good morning Sister Letitia' or whoever it was. She'd be doing hard time today for some of the crap she pulled, slapping kids around."

When my mother was a young girl Sister Letitia had accused her of doing something she did not and made her do push-ups in front of the class. When she giggles (because the other children are giggling at her because she doesn't know how to do push-ups) Sister Letitia calls my grandmother at work (my grandmother took outside sewing jobs to bring in money) and told her to come to the school. My grandmother arrived and Sister Letitia told her what my mother had done. And my grandmother said don't you ever call me at work to come down here for nothing again and with that left.

"She was the sweetest person in the world but she didn't put up with nonsense," my aunt says. And as lunch goes on and on and we now sip our teas they tell me stories about their mother. About how she took care of people in the neighborhood. How she watched out for everyone. Was kind to everyone. There are stories of taking in lost children, breaking up street fights, the sewing she took in for her friends and did ill from her bed the last months she was alive. And then my aunt asks my mother if she remembers Tommy. My mother thinks and then does remember.

"There was an old woman who lived in our build-ing who had no family except for a nephew," my aunt explains. "And her nephew, Tommy, used to come once a week and take care of her. Nobody else came to see her. Well, Tommy danced in a gay revue, wore makeup—"

"Wait," I say, interrupting. "He was a drag queen?"

Again, they consider. "I guess," she says. "I guess it was something like that. Well, one day Tommy comes to see his aunt while we're outside with Mom and these kids came up to him and started calling him names. They were going to beat him up. And Mom started yelling at them, told them to get out of here, do you remember, Felicia?" My mother nods. "She didn't like that," Aunt Santa continues, her tone serious. "Tommy was the only one who took care of his aunt. He was a good person. Our mother would not tolerate him being treated like that. She liked Tommy." This must've been the early 1950s. There was very little tolerance for gay men, much less gay men who wore makeup, when I was growing up in the '70s and '80s. I can't imagine what it was like then, in the early '50s. My aunt tosses off this story, it's one among many, but I don't know if she realizes how much it means to me. I hope it happened exactly as she says it did. It feels like the most concrete message I've ever got-ten from my grandmother. Like all of my instincts were right all along. That not only would she have accepted me, she would have fought for me, celebrated me even. Sometimes there is a strength inside me and I don't know where it comes from. But perhaps it was a gift. Something she gave to me. Something passed between us as she was exiting this world and I was entering it. At least that's what I'd like to believe.

After lunch I walk my aunt to the car that waits to take her back to New Jersey. I continue walking with my mother to Macy's. It is spring. And it is beautiful.

# Movies

WHEN I'M NINE YEARS OLD MY MOTHER TAKES me and my sister to the UA Quartet on Northern Boulevard to see *Jaws*. You have to get there early because every showing is sold out. I don't know if you'd take a nine-year-old today to see *Jaws*, but in the '70s no one gave a shit. We saw everything my mother wanted to see. As far as I was concerned this was a family film. It was so horrifying at one point that I hid on the ground and could only watch between the seats in front of me. My mother asked if I wanted to leave. "Leave?! Are you out of your fucking mind?!" This was the highlight of my life up until that point. I loved being terrified. That same year she takes me to see *The Stepford Wives*. Women are killed and turned into robots and the entire cast is dead by the end of the film. I loved it. There was never any "Hmm, maybe this isn't appropriate for a nine-year-old" from her. And thank God. My mother wasn't the kind of mother to take you to *Pinocchio* but she would take you to *The Omen*. You didn't talk about processing what you saw after or how it made you feel either. It was a fucking movie. She gave us enough credit to know that. (Also, children did not have feelings in the '70s, this was not something that was developed until much later.)

I was consumed with going to the movies, studying the film guide in the *Daily News* like the Torah. Just thinking about the ad for *The Poseidon Adventure* can to this day make the hair on the back of my neck stand on end. Getting my mother to take me always involved careful planning beforehand. "I hear this new Alfred Hitchcock film is supposed to be really something," I say to her while memorizing the screening times for *Family Plot*. (This will be Hitchcock's last film and stars Karen Black of *Airport '75*. One of the best disaster movies of all time. "The stewardess is flying the plane!" remains one of the more iconic lines in cinema history.)

"Oh," my mother would say half-interested. "Who's in it?" I'd run down the bio of the cast, summarize the plot, and give her my own take on early reviews. I was our family's Rotten Tomatoes. "That could be fun," she'd say. But if I'd add there's a show in fifteen minutes we can just make, she'd see right through me. "We're not going to the movies in fifteen minutes," she'd say. As if it were the most ridiculous thing a person could propose. You'd think I asked her to go trekking in Nepal. I had to play it just so. Wait a day. And then maybe, "It's supposed to rain on Saturday. That could be a good day to see that movie you wanted to go to."

"We'll see," she'd say. And then I'd have to let that sit for a few days.

Then on Friday: "The movie's on at 1:10 and 3:25 tomorrow, which one should we go to?"

"What movie?"

"*Family Plot.*"

"I never said we were going to that."

"Yes, you did."

"I said we'll see."

And this played out exactly the same way with dozens of movies throughout the years. And sometimes "we'll see" meant yes and sometimes it meant no. I have to hand it to my mother, she was not easily manipulated and she had no qualms in shutting down a seven-year-old whose only desire was to see *Battle for the Planet of the Apes*. It made going to the movie that much more thrilling knowing it so easily could have gone the other way. The excitement I felt sitting in the theater was matched in intensity only by its inverse reaction the times she said no. A crushing depression that could cripple me for days. During my childhood I was basically on the same emotional roller-coaster as a heroin addict. The highs were very high and the lows were really low.

Other times I'd go to the movies with my sister or our neighbor Carol Ann, who was my sister's age. But even they would be hard to convince. Carol Ann shared my taste in horror films, and when a new one came out I'd have to beg her to go with me. "My dad will drive us *and* pick us up." More often than not she'd say no. Nobody was interested in going to the movies as much as I was. Eventually I just started going alone. (But a scary movie alone, even today, is no fun.) I felt it was something I had to keep to myself, this obsession. There was something not right about it. Another thing that made me other. And I couldn't afford one more of those. As much as I seemed to love movies to everyone around me, like an iceberg, 90 percent more was underneath the surface. But I was good at hiding things. Most of what I liked, who I was, I knew from the earliest age, was not something to be shared. Everything about me felt a bit off. A bit wrong. The things I liked, I liked too much. The things I didn't, all other boys did.

(My favorite theater was the RKO Keith's in Flushing. It was one of the most impressive movie palaces in New York, originally built in the '20s as a vaudeville house and cinema. Mae West and Judy Garland performed there. Premieres were held there. Celebrities arrived in limousines. Of course I knew none of this as a child. In the '70s its glory days were already far behind it. By the time I start going it's a triplex. Two smaller theaters on the main floor and an enormous one that you had to climb a gigantic horseshoe staircase to reach. In the middle of it all was an ornate fountain. The theater had not been kept up and as a result had a Grey Gardens crumbling grandeur to it. I see *The Amityville Horror* there, and it feels as though not only the house in the film, but the theater itself, is haunted. Everything that was once beautiful, but no longer is, has a sadness to it. I see pictures of what the RKO Keith's originally looked like only many years later when I accidentally come across them online. And it's breathtaking. We tramped up and down one of the grandest theater staircases ever built, dropping popcorn, spilling soda, without a thought for any of it. Judy Garland sang there for fuck's sake! (It's also where I see my first on-screen penis after sneaking into *American Gigolo*. As far as penises go, Richard Gere's was a very good first penis.) RKO Keith's closes in the '80s. Nobody cares. The shell of the building still stands, rotting. Like the upside-down *Poseidon* at the bottom of the ocean floor.)

When I'm eleven *Star Wars* opens. It's playing at only two theaters. One in Manhattan and one on Long Island. Movies didn't always go immediately into wide release then. They would tease them out for weeks, months, build word of mouth. Today something comes out on Netflix on Friday and it's forgotten by Monday. But *Star Wars* ran for over a year. It just became part of the fabric of your life after a while. Like another family member. When something hit it big in pop culture then it stayed around a long time. Getting picked apart till every bit of marrow had been sucked from its bones.

*Star Wars* was such a thing that my father took me to see it on Long Island long before it even came to Queens. We drove out to UA Cinema 150 in Syosset, and I had never seen a line that long for a movie. I was certain my father would not want to wait. He didn't often take me to the movies and when he did, it was an event. We waited in line for the next showing. The one we wanted to see was already sold out. This was incredible, that my father would do this, I had never seen him wait in line for a movie much less for two hours. And he seemed happy to be doing it. When we were finally in the lobby they sold programs. And my dad bought me one. A program for a movie?! What the fuck was this?! I can still remember the feeling of watching that movie, having never seen anything like it before. I felt at once so small and so big. It expanded what could be. And I noticed, sitting in that theater, looking out at the crowd, that there were other fathers and sons there, too. Lots of them. And they all seemed as excited as I did. And for that day I was like everyone else. I kept the program for years. It's long gone now though.

# Village Bath Club

WHEN I'M TEN YEARS OLD WE JOIN THE VILLAGE Bath Club in Manhasset. It's a pool and tennis courts, snack bar and a restaurant. (A restaurant we never go to. Never even step foot inside. It is expensive and costs extra.) This is prompted mostly by the fact that I won't leave the house in summer. Preferring to sit in the dark cool of the basement and watch TV for those brief months of relief between school years. But my mother was insistent that I enjoy the outdoors, so, during the week, while she was at work in the city, my father would drive me and my sister to the Village Bath Club and drop us off for the day.

I would spend most of the time wandering the shopping center that was across the street, getting an ice cream at Swensen's, picking over the racks at B. Altman, poking in and out of shops like a bored housewife while my sister swam and did summer stuff. I had never heard of the Village Bath Club before we started going. Never even been much to Manhasset. But I can tell shortly after we join, by the way we're treated by everyone else, that we don't quite belong. That we're not one of them. We are from Queens and this is Manhasset, Long Island. I hadn't ever given much thought to people who might have had more than we did. Everyone we knew had roughly the same. It's not like these people in Manhasset were Kennedys or Rockefellers. But they had nicer houses, and bigger yards, and well, more money. We never discussed this either. This odd thing, this place we went every summer where we were outsiders.

They all talked to each other. All knew each other. Socialized together. These are the people who go to the restaurant. Order bottles of wine for lunch. I see them through the large dining room windows that face the pool. We only talked to the two other families we knew there who were also from Queens. My sister, always more outgoing, chatted with some of the other girls, but even she, after a while, kept her distance. I am always happy to avoid any unnecessary social interaction anyway. There could be no social anxiety if there were no social. I saw everything a little bit differently from then on, though. Did I want more? Did I want something I didn't have and hadn't realized it until I saw it? Maybe. There isn't a gay kid alive who, not unlike Belle, wants much more than this provincial life. I guess now with Instagram and Facebook people are immediately aware of those with more. Those who have seemingly everything. They see it all the time. But I wasn't, not really, up until that point. After that, it was always in the back of my mind: "They don't think we belong here."

I learn how to swim at the Village Bath Club our first summer as members. Up until now I have resisted any attempt to teach me. My mother was taught by being tossed into the water as a toddler, which, fortunately for me, has fallen out of fashion by the time I'm born. I am afforded swim lessons with an instructor who is missing one nipple and wears a Speedo. His name is Bill, and it is hard for me to concentrate on the lesson due to the two aforementioned descriptors. He was very patient and kind and held me up by the waist as I kicked and stared down intensely into the water, focusing solely on not looking at his crotch or missing nipple. A nipple had been there at one point, though, there was a small scar indicating where it had been. I had so many questions. None of them about swimming.

I take lessons with Bill once a week and it's slow going. Helen Keller learned to talk in less time. I couldn't quite grasp the coming-up-for-air part. I did all right while Bill was holding me up by the waist I would kill to still have and basically walking me across the pool. But the second he lets go I flop around like a very flamboyant fish. My parents tell me that if I can swim the length of the pool by the end of the summer they'll give me fifty dollars. This was the '70s, and for fifty dollars you could practically buy a house. And it was not like my parents to bribe me with money to do things that most typical boys did as a matter of course, so I needed to cash in while I could. Suddenly I started to focus. Divorcing myself from all of the distractions on Bill. (It didn't help that my head came directly up to his missing nipple. Although by this point I'd already spent so much time looking at it I was starting to think *two* looked weird.)

I get a little better and instantly develop a lifelong fixation on having a swimmer's build that only intensifies as I grow older. Some might also refer to this as body dys-morphia. This was given to all gay men in 1982 by Calvin Klein when his first underwear ad appears. (Today there are many examples of body positivity. Rightfully cele-brating all different shapes and sizes. Had this happened years earlier it would have saved me many thousands of hours at the gym.) By the end of the summer it's time for my cash grab performance. My parents watch from their loungers as Bill encourages me. I take several dra-matic deep breaths summoning Shelley Winters diving to save Gene Hackman in *The Poseidon Adventure*. ("In the water I'm a very skinny lady!" Another of the most iconic lines in cinema history.) I swim for what feels like an eternity, the pool suddenly the length of the English Channel, until finally . . . applause. My parents, my sis-ter, Bill, all clapping. I made it. And, unlike Shelly Win-ters, I don't die either. The other club members unaware of my victory, I am invisible. I don't see Bill again after this. Nor do I ever find out what happened to his other nipple. He's either old or dead now, but in my mind he's ageless, always in a Speedo, smiling, patient, showing me how to kick.

The following summer I take tennis lessons. I'm dis-covering this isn't so much a swim club as it is a boot camp. A Long Island Trojan horse, if you will. Forcing me out of the house and learning things I had never previously given a thought to. But I'm not bad at tennis. I grow up with a Ping-Pong table and this is just a larger version of that, I realize. I still can't throw a ball but I can hit one with a racquet, that's progress of some sort. You have to wear white tennis shorts to play on the courts. (There are only three contained in a large cage-like structure not far from the parking lot, but they treated it like it was Wimbledon.) I liked wearing white shorts, so I didn't mind tennis. My parents wanted me to be able to play one sport, so the least I could do was give them that. In the grand scheme of things it didn't seem too much to ask for. I would never admit I liked it though, I treated it more as a favor I was doing them. "You're welcome," I said with my eyes after every lesson.

I still swim and play tennis with the same level of competence I had then, but I'll take it.

Most of my time there, though, I spend wandering the adjacent shopping center named Miracle Mile. I roam up and down the length of it, killing the meat of the day (the hours between eleven and four are always the most brutal to get through). There's nothing more refreshing than stepping into an air-conditioned store on a New York August afternoon.

And another summer passes. And another. And now

I'm a teenager. And my sister, Maria, has a boyfriend, Marco, who comes with us as our guest on some days. He plays on the football team at our high school, St. Francis Prep. He is fit and handsome and has the easy charisma of a movie star (which is basically what he is in our high school, instantly elevating the social status of my sister, and by proxy, briefly, me). Marco treats me like an equal, a peer, he questions nothing about me. Does not act as if there is anything other at all about me. He is everything that I am not. And yet doesn't seem to notice.

(The first time we meet Marco, my sister has him over to our house for dinner. During this period of time we have a Persian cat, Checkers. Checkers is an indoor cat and does not leave the house under any circumstance. Our mother drills this into our heads repeatedly, *Clockwork Orange*–like, until finally the thought of Checkers walking on the grass was as absurd a thought as him piloting a helicopter. One time we thought he got out. I have still never seen my mother more upset than that day. I was scared for us more than for the cat.

Checkers has an odd habit of shitting in our basement bathroom sink. The basement bathroom is where we keep his litter box. Which I have to change, because my mother reads about toxoplasmosis, which is a disease women can get from cat feces that makes them unable to bear children or something. At least that's what I remember her telling me. In any case, the upshot is that I have to change the litter box every day for fifteen years. Checkers, for some reason, will only shit in the basement bathroom sink. Eventually, like anything after a long period of time, the sight becomes commonplace (see Bill's missing nipple). It was a happy surprise when I walked up to a sink that *didn't* have shit in it. This is my sister's first boyfriend, so her bringing him home for dinner is a big deal. We all like Marco instantly. It was as if she had brought a sixteen-year-old JFK Jr. home. There was no way you *weren't* going to like him. The three of us were instantly charmed, already being more solicitous of him than we ever were of Maria.

After dinner, I go to the basement with my sister and Marco to watch TV. A while later Marco excuses himself to use the bathroom. When he comes out he says he should be going. (He has his own car, which he drove here. Of course he does.) My sister walks him upstairs and I go into the bathroom, where I see Checkers' shit in the sink. I clasp my hands to my mouth and gasp as if I just stumbled upon a corpse. By the time I clean it up and get back upstairs Marco is already gone.

"Checkers shit in the sink and Marco saw it," I state simply to the three of them.

"Oh, God," my mother says going pale. Our family secret revealed to the one person we were trying to be our best selves for. But the strangest part is that he didn't say anything. Had he seen so much shit in other people's sinks that it wasn't worth commenting on? And whose shit did he think it was? There were so many unanswered questions. In truth, it was only further testament to what a gentleman he was that he would use our bathroom, come across a load of shit in the sink, and be too polite to mention it. I can't say I would've done the same if I were in his shoes.)

The summer Maria and Marco are dating he comes with us often to the Village Bath Club. We play tennis, swim, hang out. Let me say right now that this is not the tale of a closeted young jock who comes out in later years. This is a 100 percent straight guy. Which, of course, makes it all the more thrilling. I remember once being in the locker room there together and becoming paralyzed with fear. I did not know how to behave normally in a locker room, especially when in the company of a teenage Adonis. I didn't want to sully our relationship by even allowing myself to have a crush on him. We were above that, Marco and I, our brotherly bond transcending any sort of physical attraction I tell myself. He takes me to the movies once when my sister is working late at McDonald's. We see a double feature of *The Kentucky Fried Movie* and *The Groove Tube* and pass a bucket of popcorn between us. This is what it's like to have a friend, I think. He never asks me about sports or girls or anything that you'd think he would.

And all summer my sister and Marco let me hang out with them. Maria never seems bothered by the fact that I'm always around. It's almost as if she's happy for me. Isn't that lovely, I think now all this time later. When their relationship inevitably ends I take it harder than she does. *"What did I do wrong?!"*

But to have one summer where I am outdoors, not in the basement alone watching TV, and to have a friend who accepted me so simply, was enough to get me through much of what was to come. The fact that he was incredibly attractive only makes this story that much more touching.

We stay members of the Village Bath Club just a year or two longer, I think. We start going less and then Maria goes to college and money is needed for tuition. I go to college three years after her to Hofstra University on Long Island. And at the end of my senior year, when I'm twenty-two, I get a job at Hirshleifers Men's on the Miracle Mile in Manhasset. The shopping center across from the Village Bath Club. Hirshleifers Men's is a small, overpriced designer clothing store that one person would come into a day. I would sit reading a book behind the register. The owner tells me he prefers if I don't read. I have never in my life had eight hours go by more slowly. Each day would drag on like a prison sentence. Sometimes, the owner would bring by trash bags filled with his old designer clothing and I got to pick through it to see if I wanted anything, so that part was okay. But otherwise I was going slowly insane with nothing to engage my mind aside from folding the same five sweaters over and over again.

I stay a few months, saving money for my eventual move into the city. And on my lunch breaks that summer I would walk the length of Miracle Mile and pass all the stores I passed as a boy. But the Village Bath Club is now closed. The restaurant I still had never been inside remains standing, abandoned (until eventually the whole thing is demolished and replaced with more, larger stores). And as I look at it that summer, empty, forgotten, it just seems ordinary. And all those people who made me feel like we didn't belong didn't have that much more than we did, I realize. And one town over there are those who have more than they do and make them feel like shit. And on and on it goes. But I don't want to work here anymore, now selling clothes to these same people. I don't want to be on the outside anymore.

# Trip Advisor Review

I JUST GOT HOME FROM A WEEK AT YOUR BEAUTIFUL
hotel and I had the most fantastic time! Everybody was
incredible! Dan at the front desk and Samantha in guest
services and the entire housekeeping staff! Everyone felt
like family! I can't say enough good things about this
amazing property! It was all perfect! I only have a few
small quibbles that aren't even worth mentioning.

1. Every time I called down to the front desk for ice, it rang a really long time and nobody answered so I ended up drinking my Diet Coke without ice in the glass and I don't enjoy it half as much that way. Then when I *did* go down to the lobby I'd see the front desk clerks happily chatting with each other and I wanted to scream why doesn't anybody pick up the fucking phone but instead I just said, "Have a nice night, guys." And why isn't the ice replenished daily in the little ice bucket that *you* put in the room that I only notice is empty once I've *already* opened the Diet Coke? Anyway, not a big thing.

2. No matter what time of day it was whenever I needed to get back in my room *that's* when house-keeping seemed to be there. And they weren't just leaving either. I was beginning to think it was being done to punish me. Or I was on some hidden cam-era show. That's how ridiculous it got. (And on top of that, most nights they did the turndown service *before* I even left for dinner.) Can you imagine what it's like to return to your room at 2:00 P.M. to use the bathroom or just, like, take a minute for yourself and they're still cleaning it? Then I'd leave again and by the time I come back they've already done the

turndown service! It became a constant source of anxiety. I was afraid to go back to the room because I knew from the end of the hallway I'd see the special "housekeeping is in the room" thing they'd put on the doorknob and I didn't want to get irritated. Sometimes it just feels like my timing is off. Like I'm having an off day and everything is timed wrong and I can never quite get back on track. This could be related to that. Or it's not happening every day but it just *seems* like it's happening every day. Does that make any sense? Or it happened before and maybe it just happened *once* on this trip but because it's happened before it made it seem like more times. That could've also been what happened with the ice, too, now that I think about it. I guess the bottom line is I was always expecting someone to be in my room whenever I went back to it because of the accumulation of all the previous times that someone has been in my room when I returned to it over the years. And maybe it was just once that there was someone in there but it felt like many more times. I think that's what I'm getting at. Regardless, I felt anxious. Like, A LOT OF THE TIME, because of it. But they were lovely and the room was always spotless!

3. I went down to the lobby bar one night for a drink and waited forty-five minutes for someone to take my order. And when the server did finally come over he behaved as if *I* was the one who should be taking *his* order. But I just laughed and said, "No worries, it's just that I've been waiting a really long time and now I've got to leave for dinner in ten minutes so don't bother, I don't want anything now." Then the rest of my night I thought of my passive-aggressive comment. And how I didn't *really* have to leave for dinner in ten minutes and felt kind of shitty. And then I thought, why am *I* feeling shitty, I used to be a waiter, I know what it's like and I was never rude to anyone. Okay, maybe I wasn't waiting forty-five minutes, but it was still way more time than a person should have to wait. He took a long time to come over to me after he saw me give him the hand gesture that says, "Hey, hi, whenever you have a chance I'm ready to order, thanks," even though he pretended he didn't see it and made me feel stupid to the people who saw me give the hand gesture and saw him not seeing it. I'm sorry, "acting" like he didn't see it. Look, I was a waiter. I pretended not to see things all the time. So believe me, I recognize it when I see it. Or maybe he didn't really see

me. I suppose that's possible. He would have had no
way of knowing that I wasn't going to be just another
jerk. I know how many of those you have to deal
with, having been a waiter myself. I just wish I didn't
say that to him, like try to make him feel bad like
that, about it being too late to order. When it wasn't
even. It wasn't cool. And I hate that he made me
feel that way. And that I thought about it the whole
night. And that it made me feel bad. And petty. I
should've just ordered the fucking drink. Plus, he
actually seemed nice. I don't know, I guess I had just
had a day. I guess it was that.

4. On returning to my room after dinner and scanning
   your in-room entertainment system (which stinks) I
   accidentally ordered a Mark Wahlberg movie I had
   never even heard of for twenty-eight dollars. When I
   called down to the front desk to have it immediately
   taken off my bill no one answered (see 1). Anyone
   who knows me knows that I would never shell out
   twenty-eight dollars for a Mark Wahlberg movie. Yes,
   I watch several series on HBO that he inexplicably
   produces, but paying twenty-eight dollars to see him
   in a never-heard-of-before film as a working-class dad
   with little kids (he's over fifty, by the way, shouldn't

his kids be, like, thirty now?) in either an action or comedy scenario is where I draw the line. Okay, perhaps there was a second I thought it looked good. But literally the moment after I might have ordered it I realized my mistake. I didn't actually even watch half an hour of it before I turned on HGTV and watched a *House Hunters International* that I'd already seen instead. That's how bad the movie was. So I don't see why I should have to pay for it. The front desk manager could not have been less helpful when I disputed the charge. "I don't remember ordering this," I said to them. (This was their preferred pronoun and I am always happy to oblige. I go by he/him btw.) Then they said to me, "I'm sorry, it says you watched the movie." I only watched *part* of it! And how can they tell?? The charge should have at least been prorated. But I could see I was getting nowhere with them. If I'm being completely honest this one is really my fault, so disregard. I was still kind of feeling bad about the waiter from item 3.

5. My last night, as I was lying in bed trying to sleep, knowing I had to get up at 5:00 A.M. for my flight and afraid I won't get my wake-up call, I could hear my neighbors through the wall. They were having an

argument. Muffled angry voices through walls is one of my triggers. It was very aggressive and it seemed like they had both been drinking. I don't like when a man raises his voice to a woman. Thankfully she was giving as good as she got. (I should not assume their pronouns, but I had no way of knowing. This is just an educated guess.) It made me realize how odd hotels are. Just these small rooms of strangers right next to each other, stacked on top of each other. All of us pretending we are actors in a play. Putting our lives on hold as we perform our little parts. For the people in the lobby, the front desk, the hallways. These people who don't really know us. Who we can be anything for. Our lives reduced to only the items we brought with us. At first so liberating, so freeing. To arrive in a hotel room in a new city with nothing but the clothes in your bag. Who will I be? How will I be? They will all wonder who I am. What my story is. This is a new life that I am starting the moment I arrive. I can go to a restaurant and look at new people and imagine my life elsewhere. All that I would do differently. I will just start over from here. Never go back. But inevitably, after a few days or a week or a bit longer, you realize this has all been nothing but a charade. And it's becoming exhausting. It is not your real life. Not anyone's. And maybe you want to go home. And make your own bed. Watch your own TV. Pet your dog. Stop playing the character of the traveler, the businessman, the bon vivant, whoever you've invented yourself to be. Just to sit at home, with a book, a cup of tea. Something so simple. The thing I wanted to leave now the thing that I am most desperate to return to. Yes, I'd like to return to that. I'd like to return home. I'm ready. And I notice the couple next door has stopped fighting now. But I still can't fall asleep. Afraid I will wake up late and my plane will already be gone. On its way back without me. While I am left in this bed. Alone. How can someone fall asleep knowing all that? I take half a Xanax. It's the only way to quiet my mind. But I do get my wake-up call. And make my flight. Thank you.

Like I said, most everything was wonderful. It was only little, tiny things.

# Irene

S OMETIMES I'LL SPEND TEN MINUTES HIDING IN MY house waiting for my neighbors to leave just to avoid saying "hi." Longer if I have to. I'll be late. I'll miss my appointment. I'll do whatever it is I have to do in order to avoid seeing them. I can wait any of them out. On the rare occasion when I do see them and they say "I haven't seen you in a while," I always think you're only seeing me now because I miscalculated somehow. Was careless.

Didn't pull into the garage fast enough. I've moved without telling my neighbors. Not even putting a FOR SALE sign on the front lawn in order to avoid the inevitable questions. One managed to find out and asked for my email address so we could stay in touch. Who does that? We didn't socialize all the years I lived next door to you, we're certainly not going to do it now.

It's not that I'm unpleasant and don't say "hi" or answer the door on Halloween. (I do. And give good candy. But that's the one day of the year. Other than that, a ringing doorbell only means "hide!") Befriending a neighbor can only end badly. It is the residential equivalent of striking up a friendship with the person on the adjacent barstool. Complete happenstance has thrown you together. In the latter case alcohol impedes your good sense, enabling you to treat the idiot on the stool next to you like a long-lost twin. In the clear light of day, you wouldn't hold an elevator door open for this person. At least in that case you have booze as an excuse for your bad judgment, and chances are you will never see your new best friend again. It is only the one hellish night. But talk to your neighbor once and it's like feeding a raccoon. It keeps coming around. The person living next door to you is as random as the person stopped next to you at a red light. You wouldn't roll down your window and strike up a conversation with *them* would you? Besides, what are the odds that you will have anything in common other than your street name? Not good. I barely have enough in common with the person I live with.

I'm not a bad neighbor. I just take very much to heart the credo "good fences make good neighbors." Also fast-closing garage doors and big hats and sunglasses. Occasionally, in a moment of weakness, I'll find myself collecting the mail and feeling chatty and might see a neighbor and not bolt immediately back into the house. Say "good morning" even, comment on the weather. This empowers the neighbor to dig deeper. "Did you try the new Italian restaurant that just opened?" "I've been meaning to," I'll reply. "Let me know how you like it!" "I will! Have a great day!"

Now I've really done it. I will pay dearly for this mistake. I will have to avoid this person forever. Now we have unfinished business between us. They are waiting for my take on the new Italian restaurant. This will endlessly haunt me. I will grow to hate both the neighbor and the Italian restaurant. The possibility of "Hey, did you ever try that new place?" every time I set foot outside my house is almost too much to bear. And the more time that goes by somehow only makes it worse. Perhaps it would be easier to just go to the restaurant and report back and get on with my life. "It was great! Our new favorite spot!" "Now you have to try that sushi bar!" See? That's how that ends up. No, best just to stay inside. Peering from behind closed curtains until the coast is clear.

I have moved again recently and am determined not to make the same errors of the past. A momentary poor decision can lead to years of awkwardness. If you have been warm and friendly and exchanged numbers with someone in case of an emergency. Been "neighborly" as soon as you moved in, introduced yourself, most people will think this means you are the type of neighbor who will attend barbecues and help organize block parties. Not the type of neighbor who will wait in their running car on the corner for as long as it takes for you to load your kids into the SUV and head out before they'll drive up to their house.

(I *will* have a fifteen-minute conversation, one time, with my new next-door neighbor the first week I move in—getting the lay of the land in one fell swoop, "What are *they* like, who lives there, when's trash day, do they ticket here?"—and then successfully avoid them for the next ten years. Serial killers are less withholding. I still haven't ever seen the people who live on the other side of me, and if I play my cards right I never will. One time, when I am out of town, my husband, Brad, accepts a dinner invitation from the people next door. We end up having to sell the house.)

Now in theory what could be more American than making friends with your neighbor. Watching out for each other. "That car has been in front of Carla and Ed's for a while. Do we know if they have company?" "Let me go and check it out." That sort of thing. And this would be nice if life were a movie. But it's not. Neighbors are unavoidably annoying. Always leaving the house at the wrong time, always home when you are, always wanting to talk when you don't. "I'm literally so late, nice to see you!" as I drive over their feet and race to nothing. Each day exiting my house like it's a bank I just robbed. Shouting to my husband "Go, go, go!" before I've even closed the car door as we tear down the driveway.

When I was a kid, though, growing up in Queens, things were different. We moved into our house on Twenty-Fourth Street in 1970. It's October and I'm three years old and I sit in the backseat in a huge wooly sweater of my mother's because all of my things are packed away. My sister and I are excited about our new house. Most of my actual memories start from this day. A few cloudy ones exist before it, but here, from this day forward, is when they become clearer. Like someone has adjusted a knob on a television set.

Our new neighbor, Irene, comes out to greet us on the first day. While the moving truck is still unloading boxes. She will become a second mother to me. Irene lives in the split-level ranch right next door to our Cape Cod. Most of the houses on the block are either one or the other. Irene and Nick have six children. The youngest, Carol Ann, my sister's age. Nick works in the newspaper business, and we get free papers from that day forward. The *Daily News* or the *Post* always on our front stoop. Irene's house is spotless. And in summer their central air-conditioning stays on from June through September. As chilly as a movie theater. My mother and Irene strike up a quick, easy friendship. Irene is older and was the de facto matriarch of the block. Irene and Nick had lived there first. Everyone knew them. It was like we were famous by association.

The two women walk together each night after dinner several times around Bowne Park. We go on a cruise to Bermuda together (the summer Son of Sam is terrorizing New York), have the keys to each other's houses, visit briefly on holidays before we go to family. Irene comes with my mother, and together they walk me to my first day of school at St. Mel's. I sob for both of them when they leave me. When my mother begins working full-time in Manhattan, it is Irene who watches out for us. Who we check in with daily. I still know her phone number by heart. This is when all of New York City was a 212 area code and the first two digits were referred to with letters, not numbers. When the phone rings I pick it up. "Hi, Irene. Mom, it's Irene!" My mother and Irene calling each other nightly for anything. At any time. "I'm going walking with Irene," she would say hanging up.

I used to fantasize about being adopted by Irene and Nick if my parents died. Or even if they didn't. In their cool, tidy house, plastic on the sofa and the chairs. Four older brothers, always looking out for me. It was clear I wasn't like the other kids in the neighborhood. I didn't play in the street. Didn't throw a ball. Didn't share the language of other boys. But Irene's four sons, all teens and young adults by the time we move there, watched out for me. Accepted me like I was one of theirs. An understanding of sorts invisibly occurs between our families over time. They heard our fights and we heard theirs. We did not discuss these. These were houses close together. You learned how to live like that. Keeping each other's secrets.

Every day I came home from school, there was Irene, sitting on her porch. I would sit next to her and we would talk. Greeting the other neighbors as they passed. Often I didn't go inside. A lot of our time was spent on porches or standing in front of each other's houses. When my cousin Eddie and I fall through the ice at Bowne Park, it is Irene's house we go to soaking wet, where she gives us hot chocolates. When I don't feel well, when something is broken, when I have a question, when we are out of anything, it is Irene I go to. She is always there. Day after day, year after year. It is impossible to see our house and not to see it alongside Irene's house. They are entwined in my mind. I will dream sometimes, even today, that someone is chasing me and I run to Irene's house for safety.

After I move away to Los Angeles, the first question I ask my mother is "How's Irene doing?" She fills me in. She and Irene still taking their nightly walks around Bowne Park. The park that they will walk along together for forty years. So much of their lives overlapping.

When Irene knows I'm coming to visit she is waiting on the porch. I am eight, I am ten, I am twelve again. Sitting with her. We don't have to say much. My mother coming over. Sometimes Carol Ann, too. Or my sister, Maria. All of us chatting. Talking about the other neighbors. Who's moved, who's still there. Remember this? Remember that? It's very easy. It feels like something that I haven't felt since. I don't know how to name it.

I can still see Irene in their den. Watching episodes of *The Odd Couple* or *Mary Tyler Moore*. The den where they kept the fish tank with Jeffrey's snake that Carol Ann and I would feed. Where they put their Christmas tree. The den that led to the garage, which was always stacked with bundles of newspapers. It wasn't a big room, especially for such a large family. But it's where Irene would sit at the end of each day. When the kids were out, busy with their own lives, she would sit in her chair and watch TV. I could see the glow from inside our house. And knowing that she was in there, watching, made everything seem okay.

While I'm living in LA, I get a call from Carol Ann that Irene has cancer. We cry over the phone together. Toward the end, I fly home to see her. I sit with her as she lies in bed. I tell her what she means to me. We hold hands. We say the things that had always been unsaid.

My mother spends the last weeks of Irene's life visiting her bedside. My mother, always smiling, chatting, never afraid to be present for what is needed. Keeping her spirits up. Sitting with her. She is there with her almost at the very end. Beside her. Her best friend. She walks alone now, or with my father.

I visit my parents, and now they are the ones who have lived there the longest. My mother inheriting the mantle from Irene. Talking to all the neighbors. Introducing herself to the new ones. But it's not like it was. I know nothing is, but this really isn't. Irene hasn't lived next door to my parents in ages but I still can't help myself from looking for the glow of her television every time I'm home.

When I'm in my twenties, after I have come out to my parents, I wonder if my mother has told Irene yet. I feel it's important that she hears it from me. I tell her myself, one afternoon sitting on the porch together, and she tells me she knew. That she always knew. She doesn't have to say much more than that because I know how she feels about me. Our bond having formed gradually over many years. Or maybe it was on that first day. When I stepped out of the car in my mother's wooly sweater and she came over and said "hello."

# Gay Restaurant

WE USED TO HAVE GAY RESTAURANTS IN THE '90s. They're mostly gone now, though. There was one in Chelsea called Food Bar. Everyone went there. The food was terrible but it was a gay restaurant, you didn't go for the food, you went for the gay. (There were no foodies in the '90s. We didn't even know it was supposed to taste good.) Going with friends to Food Bar was as close as you could get to going to Mykonos without leaving the country. It was all gay, all the time. I don't think I ever saw a woman there except maybe through the window as she went by in a taxi. The owner was an older, attractive man who I knew a bit from the gym. On the occasions he would stop by my table to say "hi" it was as if I was in Elaine's and Elaine herself had joined me. (Elaine's was a restaurant on the Upper East Side famous for its famous patrons such as Woody Allen. Today, both Elaine and Woody Allen's career are long dead.)

A few doors down on the corner, was Eighteenth & Eighth, another gay restaurant. I would come here with my book and sit alone at the counter for lunch. Picking at a burger and fries while I read *Middlemarch* or *Anna Karenina* or something else suitably pretentious. Reading in public was my favorite pastime. Doing it at home didn't have the same thrill. Nobody could see me reading a book in my apartment so what was the point. I preferred a crowd. You wouldn't sing an aria to the couch, would you? I felt similarly about reading. Why waste it on no one? I was more caught up with *how* I looked reading the book than I was with the actual book. Always aware as I turned each page to put on a good show. Laugh just enough to indicate that I'm trying *not* to laugh in public. Look intently at each page, maybe

adorably bite my lip in concentration at certain pas-
sages. Let a lock of hair occasionally fall into my eyes
that I have to distractedly brush away. And make all of it
seem completely natural. As if I'm so immersed in my
book that I'm not at all aware of my surroundings. Even
though I've clocked each person in the restaurant. Every
gesture, every look, every tilt of the head is carefully considered for utmost effect. Meryl Streep put less thought
into her performance as Karen Silkwood than I did as
"person at counter with book."

When the waiter would ask if everything was okay, I
would respond startled, as if I had been abruptly woken
from a dream, "Where am I?" my eyes said. Then, after I
collect myself, "Oh, hi, I'm okay thanks." Sometimes I'd
get from the waiter "pretty good book, huh?" but usually
nothing. I don't know who I thought I was impressing
but I took my act with me throughout the city. On the
subway, waiting in line, sitting on a bench, lying out in
Sheep Meadow in Central Park (the gay beach for those
too poor to afford Fire Island). This is a touring production that shows no sign of closing. Alone at home I'd just
as soon turn on the TV than pick up a book. But plunk
me anywhere with an audience of at least one and I was
the most ravenous reader who ever existed. Unable to
stand waiting even ten seconds for a deli coffee without

at least skimming a paragraph. (There was no Starbucks then. We didn't have a lot of places to sit free like you do now. The entire city was a constant game of musical chairs. Ten seats for seven million people.)

But there was nowhere I enjoyed reading more than the counter of Eighteenth & Eighth. There was a waiter who worked there who was also a fireman. Italian and beautiful he also modeled part-time and lived in the Bronx I heard him tell someone once. It turns out a gym-built fireman/waiter-model is my ideal type. Hopefully, his ideal type is the kind of lunatic who sits at the counter in an NYU tank top reading Proust as if he were in a university library instead of the gay nexus of the world. The vibe I'm going for apparently both slut and scholar. I'm a good time, but not *too* much of a good time. The kind of girl you can take home to Mom. (If Mom is, you know, cool with everything.)

But my fireman-waiter is as friendly to me as he is to all the other customers. My minimal charms do not seduce him. Or anyone there. They are all there for fun—to drink, shriek, be silly, kiss their boyfriends. All the things you can do in a gay restaurant and not anywhere else. I'm a buzzkill with my book the size of a microwave. I don't realize this at the time. Too busy being hopeful that someone will turn to me and say

"How's the book?" or "Oh, I loved that! Would you want to go out sometime?" And that this someone will be a soap star or an Olympian or a fireman-waiter.

Positioning myself around the city with a book becomes an exhausting side job. Playing out in my head interactions that never occur. Endless compliments tossed my way like coins in a fountain. How is one supposed to concentrate on what they're reading when they also have to imagine a parallel life playing out simultaneously? One where they are approached by a well-read handsome stranger with a house in the Hamptons. Or just someone cute and nice who likes me.

I go to the movies with a book, the theater with a book, even The Roxy with a book. (The Roxy is a club that all gays go to every Saturday night in the '90s. It is our Studio 54. I somehow manage to get on a list that entitles me to a card to get in on Saturdays without having to wait in line. Each week stepping in front of the hundreds that swarm the street with a delicate "excuse me," my arm extended holding out a golden ticket, the velvet rope automatically opening for me like supermarket doors. Getting this card is the singular most exciting thing that happens to me in my twenties. Maybe ever. I still have it. I'll show it to you if we ever meet, it's in my wallet.)

I carefully position myself with my book wherever I go. Get into my pose. Cross my legs, sip my coffee, look down at the page. Down. Down. Always looking down.

The thing that I thought would help me meet people was, of course, accomplishing the exact opposite. Why I could not see this at the time remains unclear. Too desperate to create a fantasy that no one cared about. Not even me.

I would like to go back to the gay restaurant again. I would like to be twenty-five again. I would sit at the counter with no book. Clear-eyed. Friendly. Unafraid. I would look up. And I would ask the fireman-waiter his name.

# A Chorus Line

I CAN'T OVERSTATE HOW OFTEN THE COMMERCIAL for *A Chorus Line* ran in New York in the '70s and '80s. It was on day and night. "The reason for the line outside the theater . . ." the announcer intoned, ". . . is the line *inside* the theater." FUCK YES! nine-year-old me thought every time it appeared. All the actors, side by side, headshots covering their faces *"Who am I anyway? Am I my résumé? That is a picture of a person I don't know."* (Still perhaps one of the greatest lyrics in musical theater history.) And finally, of course, all dressed in gold, tipping their top hats *"One . . . singular sensation, every little step he takes . . ."* This, along with the *Evita* commercial that ran a few years later, would change my life. (A *Chorus Line* starred Robert LuPone as Zach, the exacting choreographer, and *Evita* starred national treasure and Broadway legend Patti LuPone. I find out they are brother and sister years later and my mind is blown. Between us, my sister and I can barely entertain our relatives from New Jersey.)

I saw the actors in the commercial so often that I began to think of them as friends. I knew all of their outfits, the little bits from their solos, every flourish and thrust. Every twirl and jump. I wanted to see *A Chorus Line* for almost as long as I can remember being alive. When I finally do see it for the first time I'm thirteen. (Hello twelve, hello thirteen, hello love. Google it.) It's been running for years already at this point. I go with my sister, Maria, to a Wednesday matinee. We get our tickets at the TKTS booth in Times Square for half price. (The show runs without an intermission and I feel like I've been shortchanged. An intermission draws the event out, allowing you to savor it just that much longer. Now when I find out a show has no intermission my first response is "Thank fucking God, please let it be only ninety minutes." But then I wanted everything to last forever, forestalling my return to real life for as long as possible. Funny how that changes.) And I sit there watching the performers onstage, none of them from the commercial any longer, as they audition for a spot in the chorus of a Broadway musical. Their lives so glamorous to me. All I want is to audition for something. To be taken from where I am and brought somewhere else. To be auditioning for a Broadway musical, what could be more fabulous than that? Certainly not doing homework and emptying the dishwasher in Queens. To me, the people auditioning for the chorus line were the most successful people in the world. They were auditioning for BROADWAY! The idea that someone could be that successful was extraordinary to thirteen-year-old me.

I see the show many times during the course of its run, and when I'm twenty-four, I go with my roommate, Steve, who is also an aspiring actor, to the final performance. And we sit in the balcony far from the stage and we are spellbound one last time. I'm still younger than most of the people in the cast and still have absolutely no idea how one gets an audition for a Broadway show. My feelings for the show now are the same as they are the first time I see it when I'm thirteen. "One day that's going to be me auditioning for a show." And as they tip their gold hats and kick their gold legs one final time we collectively jump to our feet. We all get key chains in the shape of tickets for this last performance. A gift. For only us. (Isn't that a delightful thing to do? Something so small can stay with you for so long. I still have mine.)

When I am in high school I don't audition for any of the shows. Too afraid of doing something—anything that will draw unwanted attention. Until my senior year, that is. I am starting to become myself. It happens without me even trying. It's like I can't stop it. Some force within me knows I'm graduating soon and it doesn't give a fuck. It is rising up, gaining strength. I decide to audition for my senior musical, *South Pacific*, and am up for the role of Emile de Becque—a widowed, middle-aged French murderer who dates an annoying American nurse during World War II. I audition with the song "Pilate's Dream" from *Jesus Christ Superstar*. It falls within my range, which is approximately two notes. It's also a good fucking song. I make it through to callbacks, where I am up against several other boys. A surprising fact, since I am unable to sing. But St. Francis is not exactly the High School of Performing Arts. No one was belting out songs on lunchroom tables or dancing on taxicab roofs here. The talent pool was not that deep and apparently I'm close to the top.

As soon as the part of Emile de Becque, THE LEAD, is dangled in front of me it is all that I want. There are many other supporting roles in the musical. It is World War II after all. But I am only interested in Emile de Becque, THE LEAD.

During my callback I have to sing his big number, "Some Enchanted Evening." If you are not familiar with this song, shame on you. It is what we call a standard. Go listen to it on one of your devices. It is often performed by people such as Placido Domingo and is a particularly tricky number for someone such as myself who cannot sing. I'm not sure if I think I can sing at the time, or why I think I can sing if I *did* indeed think I could sing, but, let me state again as clearly as possible for the record, I cannot, could not, sing. Certainly not "Some Enchanted Evening." I can still see myself auditioning in front of Sister Anne, my English teacher and the musical's director. (She had a whispery, childlike voice that predated Paris Hilton by a good two decades.) My gargled strangulations as I try to hit each ever increasingly higher note.

The scary thing is that I'm not even the worst one. I'm, like, in the middle. I'm even seriously considered.

Sister Anne saves me perhaps from the greatest humiliation of my life by not casting me as the lead. I am given
the role of one of the sailors instead and my first thought
when I see the cast list is, *Fuck that*.

I am too good, my talent too undeniable, to play
some dumb sailor, some nobody. It's Emile de Becque
or nothing for me. I went from not even daring to audition to a state of outrage over not getting cast as the lead
in about a minute. (This would be unusual if I were not
gay. But for a gay it is par for the course.)

Naturally I decline the role. "No thank you, dear.
Good luck with your little show." Condescension oozing out of my every pore as I waltz out of the auditorium
like I'm fucking Jane Fonda. "Glad you're familiar with
prayers, Sister Anne, 'cause you're gonna need 'em."

By the time I get home I already feel like I've made
a mistake. Maybe it would've been fun. Maybe I should
have stayed. It's too late now as I sit in front of *One Life
to Live* and watch Viki succumb to her alternate personality, Niki, once again. I didn't even tell anyone I was
auditioning, so there's no one to tell I didn't get it. Well,
I *did* get it. But not the lead. This audition is the only
time I have stayed past the final bell in the four years
that I am at St. Francis Prep. In my yearbook, underneath my photo and name it is blank because I have

done nothing. No activities, no clubs, no sports (duh). It would have been maybe nice to do *one* thing. A sailor singing "Bloody Mary." I could have done that. A memory of singing and dancing with my classmates might have been a better one than being spiteful to a child-voiced nun. Then again, it might not have been.

Years later, when I am forty, I return to see the Broadway revival of *A Chorus Line* and it is suddenly a completely different show and I am floored. My younger self saw these dancers as accomplished and successful and already so far beyond anything in their career that I could have imagined. But at forty I realize I was wrong and I actually saw the show for what it was. People who give up everything for a measly part in the chorus. They are not famous, they are not the leads, they are struggling. And scraping. And desperate. The part means everything to them. They are not the huge successes that I originally thought they were. They are jobbing actors and dancers trying to get by. And it's heartbreaking and moving and touching in all the ways I couldn't see when I am thirteen and fourteen and sixteen and nineteen and twenty-three and twenty-four. Every musical number makes me cry because this time I can see what I could not all those other times.

When I get to college, I do audition for shows. And I

get a few parts. And I am fearless now in the way young people can be. My true self finally appearing after being hidden for so long. Like trying on a new outfit and admiring what you see in the mirror. For the first time I don't worry about what anyone thinks.

Every year at Hofstra there is a Shakespeare Festival and one of Shakespeare's plays is performed on a replica of the Globe stage. The show runs an entire week. Local high school students attend midweek matinees. It's basically a fucking Broadway run. And in my senior year, I get the seventh lead in *Twelfth Night*. I play Fabian, one of the servants in Olivia's court. I have a Scottish accent because Dr. Madden, the aged alcoholic director, thinks it will be a good idea. He also thinks my character should be elderly and walk hunched in the shape of a question mark. There is nothing in Shakespeare's play that would indicate any of this. But Shakespeare is dead and Dr. Madden is not. (Well, he is now.) The "makeup artist" draws thick crayon-like lines on my face indicating "old age." (Is there anything more touching than a young person dressed in a school show to look old? More gray, more lines! Their young body stooped and crooked, but the life force still bursting out of them like candy from a piñata.) I still remember my first line, uttered like Scotty in *Star Trek*. "There is at the gate, madam, a young gentleman who much desires to speak with you." The accent so thick it's all but unintelligible (not unlike an actual Scottish accent). My wavy black hair grayed by an entire thing of baby powder (which, I believe, is now considered asbestos), a white cloud of talcum follows me across the stage. I get a laugh off of every line. I have no jokes, mind you. This is actually known as "pulling focus" and not thought of highly by other actors. But no one knows this at the time. We are all young and stupid. College acting is basically *Survivor*. Whoever gets the most attention wins. There was not exactly a high bar for sophisticated humor at Hofstra University in the '80s. A funny accent was funny. Dr. Madden was right after all.

I don't think there has ever been a production of *Twelfth Night* before or since (and I am including the original one that Shakespeare attended) that was stolen by the character of Fabian. A character I've since seen dropped from several productions, as he's considered that inconsequential. (How do you drop the best character in the show, I'd sit there thinking after noticing Fabian's omission from the program, already prepared to hate the production.) *Twelfth Night* has about six of Shakespeare's most famous characters in it and I upstage all of them. All of my lines, basically exposition that could be given to any other character or even cut, are now show-stopping laugh lines confusing the entire company. Each of my entrances brings delight and applause. I am Kramer. And I eat it up. I live for the audience. They are my people. I perform for them and them alone. This is my *Funny Girl*, my *Hello, Dolly!*, my *Gypsy*. I feel euphoria on opening night.

"Great job," my fellow cast members say to me after the show, slightly confused. Kind of like "that wasn't supposed to happen, was it?" I am told that the critic for the *Hofstra Chronicle* is there that night and he is going to single out my performance in his review. If Frank Rich were writing about me for the *New York Times* I couldn't have been more excited. "I'm going to be in the fucking *Chronicle*! I've made it!" This is the pinnacle of my college performing career. I've been chasing the high of that opening night ever since. I had been seen for the first time. And I wanted more. More. More.

Recently, I see *A Chorus Line* again. Now I am in my fifties. (The most difficult sentence I have ever written. Until I'm in my sixties, I guess.) Look at them. To be auditioning for a Broadway musical, what could be more fabulous than that? They were artists, they were fearless. They were doing what they loved no matter what. And to me they were the most successful people in the world. I was right the first time.

# Graduation

SHORTLY AFTER I FIND OUT WHAT THE ACT OF SEX is I realize this is something I am not going to be able to accomplish with a woman. At ten years old I was already like "oh, no, no, no, that's not for me, thank you." I think, I'm ten, I'm not certain. Probably younger, probably nine. I find out what it is the same time my sister does. She is two and a half years older and immediately tells me after she hears it at school. So I must have been younger. In the bombshell department, it's right up there with finding out there is no Santa Claus.

"There's no fucking way that can be true!" I say once she tells me the specifics. And yet it was. We didn't learn about sex from our parents. No one did then. You caught bits and pieces at school or from friends. It was like someone telling you the plot of *Game of Thrones* before you've actually seen any of it. It all just sounds like a confusing mishmash of nonsense. How our parents expected us to learn about it was beyond me. I didn't ask them then and I'm not asking them now. The whole thing had a science fiction–like quality to it. It's all unsettling information. Once you know what it is, your childhood is officially over.

I had always assumed I was going to have a family, I just never took a hard look at what that was going to look like. The actual knowledge of what the act of sex consists of pretty much sends my life into a tailspin. "THIS is what you have to do when you're married?"

When I'm ten *Charlie's Angels* premieres. I am obsessed. Three beautiful women (well, *two* beautiful women and one smart one) solve crimes by posing as bikini models and beauty contestants. If I noticed the writing was stilted and hackneyed at ten, it must've been really fucking horrible. But I still loved it. Farrah

Fawcett had a very famous swimsuit poster that hung in every boy's bedroom (one word, "nipple") but it was Jaclyn Smith's poster that hung in mine. Farrah Fawcett's sexuality was too overt for ten-year-old closeted Gary, but Jaclyn Smith had just the right touch of elegance and midlevel sophistication. In her poster, Jaclyn wore a peignoir (a negligee with a light robe over it. Jesus. I shouldn't have to explain *everything* to you). Very coy and demure. Right up my alley. With the poster hanging in my room I might as well have spray painted STRAIGHT across the wall. I mean, what gay boy would have a poster of Jaclyn Smith in a peignoir on his bedroom wall? (Turns out all of them.)

In my mind, that Jaclyn Smith poster was my ticket to a normal family. I had it all planned out almost from the first time I saw her holding a gun in her white two-piece. She would make the perfect wife I decided. Beautiful and kind, we would one day marry. And on our wedding night we would have sex. Now this was the most difficult part of my fantasy to pull off. But if I really put my mind to it I could do it, I tell myself. If only just once. I would use drugs and drink and mind control and anything else at my disposal to just jam it in there one time. And the day after our wedding I would be called away for work (something that involved a

slim-fitting Italian suit and a briefcase and a first-class
flight with lowball glasses and clinking ice cubes) and
when I would return Jaclyn, my wife, would be pregnant
from our one night together (which, again, I wasn't sure
I could pull off but was determined to make happen at
any cost), and we wouldn't have sex again because, well,
she was pregnant and I didn't know that was a thing you
did when you were pregnant. I'm only ten for Christ's
sake! She would give birth to a beautiful baby (boy or
girl, didn't matter, as long as it was healthy, blah blah)
that we would bring home from the hospital together.
Our perfect family.

And the next day Jaclyn would die in a car accident.
I pictured it going off a cliff, we live in LA. Now I had
a child and no wife. And I would never love anyone
again. (Which was totally understandable, being that I
was married to Jaclyn Smith, the most beautiful woman
in the world.) And I would never have to date or pretend or be the object of rumor or innuendo. I would
be above reproach. Forever bemoaning my lost love.
Like Heathcliff in *Wuthering Heights*. Only not insane.
I would be pitied but I would soldier on for my baby boy
(I guess it's a boy) and everyone would say, "There goes
Gary and little Matthew (his name is Matthew), doesn't
the baby look just like his mother. Or his father. They're

both so gorgeous. There was never a love stronger than that of Gary and Jaclyn Smith. So sad. He's so young and beautiful. But obviously he's never going to be with another woman again."

This is how I decided nobody would ever suspect me of being gay and I would still get to have kids (the only glitch, again, having to have straight sex one time, which was not an inconsiderable fly in the ointment). Looking back now it was an idea not without its flaws, but I was committed to it. (To this day I still think of Jaclyn Smith as the one who got away. Sorry, Brad.) Now, of course, today gays can have kids any number of ways. Surrogates, adoption, some other combination or another. They typically have twins or triplets at the drop of a hat now. But then, in the '70s, I felt my only option was marrying Jaclyn Smith, having sex with her once (somehow), and then sending her off a cliff to her fiery death. As plans go, it's not great.

Today, though, the thought of having a child is terrifying. I don't want a teenager when I'm seventy. I don't have the resources of an Elton John. The child will no doubt grow into a teen who will lie and do drugs and leave me at home confused at an age where I am unable to use any of the future technology. I've seen *Euphoria*. And teenagers will only get worse as time goes on.

No, thanks, I'm not equipped to deal with whatever the fuck is coming down the road after TikTok. Teenagers frighten me. I will cross the street to avoid a gathering of more than two. Head down as I quickly shuffle by. My time to have a child is past. They came out with all this shit a little too late for me. I mean it would be nice to have one for Instagram, but otherwise, I'm good. Sometimes I think perhaps I've made an awful mistake and I'm missing out on the most extraordinary experience in life, but then I read about a drug-addicted celebrity's child and feel much better. Besides, things don't always work out the way you think they're going to when you're young. They usually don't.

I realize when I get to high school that marrying Jaclyn Smith is not going to be the free pass that I had previously thought. I adopt a new plan. My best chance to avoid any suspicion, any unwanted attention, is to talk to as few people as possible. To blend in. Disappear. In four years I don't eat lunch in the cafeteria once. I read Stephen King novels in the library, my friends are Carrie and vampires and a killer Plymouth Fury. I wander out of the building and go for walks to nearby Bagel Nosh or Bloomingdale's. Studying people. Preparing myself for a life that I am not yet living. Taking notes.

Information that I tuck away for future use. I bide my time. I wait. And I wait. And I wait.

My senior year arrives and I am in art class. Our teacher is a lay teacher. This is what we call the teachers in a Catholic school who are not nuns or brothers but just regular people. And now, thinking about it, I'm pretty sure she was a lesbian. Not just because she had very short hair, but that does heavily factor into it. We are working on a project, the class is comprised of juniors and seniors, and there is an announcement over the PA for all the seniors to gather on the football field to have their senior photo taken. The seniors in my art class get up to leave and I remain behind with the juniors, continuing to work on my shitty art project.

And this teacher (the one I'm pretty sure now was a lesbian) comes up to me, I no longer remember her name but I remember this moment, and she says "Aren't you going to have your picture taken?" And I tell her "No." She is very kind now. And speaks to me softly so the others can't hear.

"I think if you don't have your picture taken with the class you're going to regret it one day." And I look at her and say with certainty, "I promise you, I won't."

And with that she walks away. I wonder sometimes

if she was right after all. But I don't have my yearbook anyway. It's gone, I don't know where. So what does it really matter?

A few weeks before graduation, my parents talk to me. My dad tells me he and my mom have an opportunity to go on a cruise to Alaska but it falls during the day of my graduation ceremony. The cruise line my dad works for often only lets us know last minute when there is available space on a trip. My parents tell me they won't go if I'd rather they attend my graduation. But this somehow feels right to me. I don't need witnesses to the nothing I've made of these last four years. This is something I need to see through on my own. Like signing divorce papers. It's all too fitting, really. My happiest moments of the last years have all taken place on cruise ships anyway. The most perfect nights always the second-to-last ones. When they turn the lights off in the dining room and all the waiters enter with Baked Alaskas held high over their heads, each one filled with sparklers. The reggae song "You Can Get It If You Really Want" plays over the sound system. The mood is nothing short of total bliss. My sister and I always looking to single out our waiter until he arrives at our table and shows off the Baked Alaska to us like a Fabergé egg as everyone sings along.

"*You can get it if you really want/ but you must try/ try and try/ try and try/ You succeed at last.*"

It is exhilarating and magical and everything my life in Queens is not.

And now my parents get to go to the actual Alaska. Yes, please go to the birthplace of the dessert that has given me so many happy memories while I wrap things up here. My mother makes me promise not to use her car while she's away. It is a Mustang and she fucking loves that car. So on the day of my high school graduation I take a taxi with my sister to St. Francis Prep. Both of us dressed nicely. I am glad to have her with me. It is okay that she sees I have no friends. But *she* is my friend and we are going together. The driver tells us he has to make one stop on our way to pick up two more people also going to the ceremony. And he pulls up to a house, not unlike our own, and a classmate of mine, Geraldine Eidenwanger and her brother, Wallace, get in. Geraldine had gone to grammar school with me as well, and we were friendly, and her older brother, Wallace, had gone to school with my sister and now they were both in the same taxi as we were.

I'm embarrassed for Geraldine to see me going to graduation alone with my sister and it doesn't occur to me that she is doing the exact same thing with her brother. What her circumstances were that also brought the two of them together with us in this taxi I have no idea. Too concerned always with how I appeared to other people. All four of us were quiet. Like we knew this was strange but didn't know why. I wish we could have laughed about it. Been silly. Something. Instead we exchange congratulations and go our separate ways as soon as we step out of the car. I never see Geraldine again. Not even later on that day. We share a silent taxi ride and nothing else.

I don't remember any of the ceremony. I couldn't tell you if it was inside or outside. I remember considering not even going at the last minute, but my sister, Maria, helps convince me, and yes she is right, I need to finish this. Cross every *t*, dot every *i*. Only by graduating can I finally close this chapter and move on. I don't know why I feel this way but I know it to be true. After it's over I find my sister. I can still see the dress she is wearing. There are flowers on it. We have no pictures from this day. Maria leaves from the ceremony to go to work, or meet friends, I don't remember where, but I am alone. That I know. I walk to the bus stop that is across the street from the school and wait for the Q76, the bus I have boarded every day the last four years at exactly 2:37, the time of the final bell.

But there are no other kids on the bus this day. They

are with their families and friends. Off to parties and lunches. I don't want to be with them, though. Don't feel like I'm missing anything. I want to be here on this bus alone, pulling away from this school for one last time. I sit in the empty bus thinking, now my life will begin.

The lights go out and the waiters enter with Baked Alaskas held high over their heads. The dining room lit by hundreds of sparklers. My heart is racing.

# I'd Like to Thank

My nieces, Emily Abeshouse and Sarah Abeshouse, for making me feel like I'm never missing out on kids because I've got them.

My sister, Maria Abeshouse and brother-in-law Adam Abeshouse, for always being there, in good times and in tan.

Sal Messina and Steve Hasley, who appear briefly in

these pages but not briefly in my life, for their many, many, many years of friendship.

My aunt, Santa Gaines, for so generously and lovingly telling the story of my grandmother.

My neighbor from over fifty years ago, Carol Ann McCauley, for sharing her mother, Irene, with me. And for going with me to see *Friday the 13th* in 1980. I still appreciate it.

My agents Jay Sures and Albert Lee at UTA for being so terrific.

Tony Peyrot for his continued guidance and friendship.

The super-talented Alasdair McLellan for his photo of me for this book jacket.

At Audere Media, Aileen Boyle, and everyone at Holt: Maggie Richards, Catryn Silbersack, Hannah Campbell, Meryl Levavi, Allison Carney, Lori Kusatzky and, most of all, Amy Einhorn for everything.

James Melia, my brilliant editor and friend, for being the best, most wonderful reader a fella could have.

Mom and Dad for always wanting more for me.

And Brad for being more.

## About the Author

**Gary Janetti** is the bestselling author of *Do You Mind If I Cancel?* and writer and producer of *Family Guy, Will & Grace, Vicious,* and *The Prince*. He lives in Los Angeles.